THE
CAST
IRON

THE CAST IRON

• 13-Digit ISBN: 978-1-40034-045-3 • 10-Digit ISBN: 1-40034-045-4 • This book may be ordered by mail from the publisher. Please include $5.99 for postage and handling. • Please support your local bookseller first! • Books published by Cider Mill Press Book Publishers are available at special discounts for bulk purchases in the United States by corporations, institutions, and other organizations. For more information, please contact the publisher. • Cider Mill Press Book Publishers • "Where good books are ready for press" • 501 Nelson Place • Nashville, Tennessee 37214 • Visit us online at cidermillpress.com • Typography: Freight Sans Pro, Freight Big Pro, Freight Text Pro • Printed in Malaysia • 24 25 26 27 28 OFF 5 4 3 2 1 • First Edition

THE
CAST
IRON

100+ RECIPES FOR EVERYONE,
FROM THE WORLD'S BEST CHEFS

CIDER MILL
PRESS

BOOK
PUBLISHERS

CONTENTS

INTRODUCTION

As comfortable on the stovetop as it is in the oven or over a campfire, and capable of turning out everything from a hearty stew whose rich flavor is the result of a lengthy braise in the oven to an airy pastry and a beautifully burnished steak, it's fair to wonder how kitchen supply stores convince people to purchase anything other than cast iron. Somehow, it is not outlandish to claim that one could not have another piece of cookware in the house other than a cast-iron skillet and still do splendidly in the kitchen.

Home cooks everywhere seem to be in agreement, as they turn to cast iron when preparing meal after meal, and hand down these durable, versatile, dependable, and handsome implements through their families for generations.

But those home cooks aren't the only devotees—in fact, the world's very best chefs are as big of fans of cast iron as anyone, turning to its unparalleled heat-conducting abilities to pull off some of their most exciting preparations, relying on its versatility to save seconds that are invaluable in the hyper-demanding service industry, and counting on its durability to withstand the inevitable beating every implement in a professional kitchen undergoes and cut down on costs.

Preserving cast iron's numerous good qualities is dependent on a little TLC, however, as cast-iron cookware is only as good as its level of seasoning. This coating of polymerized oil allows cast iron to remain nonstick and prevents it from rusting. It is not difficult to maintain a proper level of seasoning, but it does require some devotion and consistency after the cookware has been used. First off, while many devotees claim that soap should never touch a piece of cast iron, the truth is that if your seasoning is on point, a little bit of soap is OK to use in particularly gritty preparations. But for the most part, a little bit of water and a sponge or a brush with plastic bristles will suffice to clean off the cookware. Once that step has been accomplished, cast iron needs to be thoroughly dried and rubbed with a little bit of canola, avocado, or vegetable oil to ensure it remains in good condition.

Do that, and the sky is the limit for what cast iron can do in the kitchen, as each and every page of this book proves.

A collection of cast-iron recipes from the world's best chefs, it brings some of the brightest lights from the modern culinary movement right into your home. From the genteel-yet-rustic flavors that made Erin French a household name and the approachable complexity Sean Brock used to revitalize Southern cooking, to the dynamic fusions of Edward Lee and the edgy elegance of Gabrielle Hamilton, a thoughtful trip through this book is as good as a year in culinary school, guaranteed to refine your palate, hone your skills, and spur your imagination.

APPETIZERS
& SIDES

Whether it is being counted upon to supply the heat needed to properly fry an ingredient or add just a hint of char to a wholesome side, cast iron always comes through. Its ability to supply dishes that will round out your table, and make the most of each ingredient has never been in doubt, but in the hands of the world's very best chefs, its potential to turn each and every meal into an occasion hits new heights.

Torta al Testo

One of the oldest Italian focaccia, this gets its name from the pan it is traditionally cooked in. Luckily, a cast-iron skillet is a more than capable substitute for the testo.

17.6 oz. all-purpose flour, plus more as needed

1 teaspoon fine sea salt

1 teaspoon baking soda

8.8 oz. water

1. In a large bowl, combine the flour, salt, and baking soda. Incorporate the water gradually and work the mixture until it comes together. If kneading by hand, transfer the dough to a flour-dusted work surface. Work it until it is compact, smooth, and elastic. Divide the dough into 2 pieces and shape each piece into a ball. Cover the balls with plastic wrap and let them rest at room temperature for 30 minutes.

2. Warm a medium cast-iron skillet over medium heat. Using a rolling pin, flatten each ball until it is a disk that is approximately ¼ inch thick. Use a fork to poke holes in the disks.

3. Working with 1 disk at a time, place it in the pan and cook until it is golden brown all over, about 6 minutes per side.

4. Cut the cooked focaccia into wedges. These can be enjoyed as is, or filled with cold cuts, cheese, or sautéed vegetables.

Bibingka

Bibingka is a popular breakfast or merienda (snack) food in the Philippines. Traditionally, it's placed in a banana leaf–lined terra-cotta pot and baked in a clay oven with preheated coals, but cast iron's unique ability to conduct and distribute heat makes this preparation accessible to all.

---

1 banana leaf, washed and dried

1 cup sweet rice flour

¾ cup sugar

1 tablespoon baking powder

½ teaspoon fine sea salt

1 cup whole milk

½ cup coconut milk

3 large eggs

3 tablespoons unsalted butter, melted, browned, and cooled

Cured Egg Yolks (see page 200), grated, for garnish

Parmesan cheese or Edam cheese, grated, for garnish

1. Preheat the oven to 375°F.

2. Cut the banana leaf into squares and line a medium cast-iron skillet with them, making sure to overlap the squares. Trim any pieces that rise above the lip of the pan.

3. Combine the rice flour, sugar, baking powder, and salt in one bowl and the milk, coconut milk, eggs, and melted butter in another.

4. Combine the mixtures, stir until they form a smooth batter, and let the batter sit for 20 minutes to fully hydrate the flour.

5. Pour the batter into the banana leaf–lined skillet, place in the oven, and bake until a toothpick inserted into the center comes out clean, about 30 minutes. Remove and let it cool slightly.

6. When the cake has cooled, garnish with the Cured Egg Yolks and cheese and serve.

Bibingka
see page 11

Skillet Cornbread

Full of flavor thanks to the spices, and subtly but surprisingly rich thanks to the ricotta and buttermilk, you won't hear anyone complaining if you decide to show up to the family barbecue with this cornbread.

½ cup unsalted butter

3 eggs

2 tablespoons brown sugar

1 cup cornmeal

1 cup all-purpose flour

1 tablespoon baking powder

1½ teaspoons fine sea salt

½ teaspoon mustard powder

1 teaspoon chili powder

½ cup honey

1 cup buttermilk

2 tablespoons whole-milk ricotta cheese

1. Place the butter in a large skillet and melt it over medium heat. Cook the butter until it starts to brown and give off a nutty aroma. Remove the pan from heat and let the brown butter cool completely.

2. Preheat the oven to 325°F and position a rack in the center. Coat a large cast-iron skillet with nonstick cooking spray.

3. Place the eggs and brown sugar in the work bowl of a stand mixer fitted with the whisk attachment and whisk on high until the mixture is pale and fluffy.

4. Place the cornmeal, flour, baking powder, salt, mustard powder, and chili powder in a mixing bowl, stir to combine, and set the mixture aside.

5. Add the brown butter, honey, buttermilk, and ricotta to the stand mixer's work bowl and whisk until incorporated. Add the dry mixture and whisk until the mixture comes together as a smooth batter.

6. Pour the batter into the skillet and place it in the oven. Bake until a cake tester inserted into the center of the cornbread comes out clean, about 35 minutes.

7. Remove the cornbread from the oven and invert it onto a wire rack. Let the cornbread cool slightly before slicing and serving.

Spoon Rolls

A cast-iron minicake pan is the perfect baking vessel for these home-made spoon rolls, a recipe passed down through the ultimate cast-iron dynasty, the Lodge family, for generations.

1 packet of active dry yeast

2 cups lukewarm water (90°F)

¼ cup sugar

1 large egg, beaten

¾ cup unsalted butter, melted

4 cups self-rising flour

1. Preheat the oven to 400°F. Grease the wells of 2 cast-iron minicake pans or cast-iron muffin pans.

2. In a large bowl, dissolve the yeast in the warm water and let the mixture sit until it starts to foam.

3. Add the remaining ingredients and stir until a smooth batter forms.

4. Spoon the batter into the prepared pans, filling each well halfway to two-thirds full. Any unused batter will keep in an airtight container in the refrigerator for up to 1 week.

5. Place the rolls in the oven and bake until they are puffy and golden brown, about 20 minutes. Remove from the oven, invert the pans to turn the rolls out onto a wire rack, and briefly cool before serving.

New Potato Confit

New potatoes are sweeter than their more mature counterparts, since the sugars haven't had time to develop into starches.

---

4 cups canola oil

5 lbs. new potatoes

Salt and pepper, to taste

1. Place the canola oil in a cast-iron Dutch oven and warm it to 200°F over medium heat.

2. While the oil is warming, rinse and scrub the potatoes and then pat them dry. Carefully slip the potatoes into the warm oil and cook until fork-tender, about 1 hour.

3. Drain the potatoes, season generously with salt and pepper, and stir to ensure that the potatoes are evenly coated. Enjoy warm or at room temperature.

YIELD: 2 Servings / **ACTIVE TIME:** 10 Minutes / **TOTAL TIME:** 25 Minutes

Baby Bok Choy with Salsa Macha

Bok choy's crunchy stalk, leafy greens, and subtle grassy, peppery flavor allow one to utilize a number of techniques in preparing it, but blanching it first helps bring out its vibrant green color.

Salt and pepper, to taste

4 baby bok choy, trimmed and halved lengthwise

2 tablespoons extra-virgin olive oil

2 cups oyster mushrooms, sliced

1 red bell pepper, stem and seeds removed, sliced

1 small onion, sliced

½ cup Salsa Macha (see page 231)

1. Bring water to a boil in a large saucepan and prepare an ice bath. Add salt until the water tastes like seawater. Add the bok choy and cook until it is just tender, about 2 minutes. Drain the bok choy, plunge it into the ice bath, and drain again. Transfer the bok choy to a paper towel–lined plate and let it dry.

2. Place the olive oil in a large cast-iron skillet and warm it over medium heat. Add the mushrooms, season them with salt and pepper, and cook, stirring occasionally, until they are browned, 10 to 12 minutes.

3. Add the pepper and onion and cook, stirring occasionally, until they are tender, about 8 minutes.

4. Stir in the bok choy and cook until it is warmed through. Transfer the vegetables to a serving dish, drizzle the Salsa Macha over the top, and serve.

YIELD: 6 Servings / ACTIVE TIME: 15 Minutes / TOTAL TIME: 30 Minutes

Spring Bread Salad with Asparagus, Radishes, Peas & Mint

Seek out a good white bread like a country bâtard or other crusty sourdough loaf for this recipe—something made with a good, long ferment that gives it a rich and sour flavor.

---

1 lb. asparagus

3 tablespoons extra-virgin olive oil

Salt and pepper, to taste

1 cup shelled fresh peas, blanched

2 bunches of mixed radishes (such as French breakfast and any other beautiful radishes that catch your eye), halved

3 cups torn bread pieces

2 tablespoons chopped fresh mint

2 cups pea tendrils or pea shoots

3 tablespoons Macerated Shallot Vinaigrette (see page 245)

Fresh chives, for garnish

1. Preheat the oven to 425°F.

2. Cut the asparagus into 2-inch pieces, discarding the tough ends. Arrange the pieces in a single layer on the baking sheet, drizzle with 1 tablespoon of olive oil, and season with salt and pepper. Give the pan a shake to coat the asparagus. Roast until pieces are tender but still a bit crunchy, about 5 minutes. Set aside to cool to room temperature.

3. Combine the asparagus, peas, and radishes in a medium bowl.

4. Heat a medium cast-iron skillet over medium-high heat, then pour in the remaining 2 tablespoons of olive oil. When the oil shimmers, add the bread and cook, turning partway through, until browned, about 4 minutes. Add to the vegetable mixture.

5. Sprinkle in the mint, pea tendrils, and the vinaigrette and toss to dress. Season with more salt and pepper if desired and garnish with a flurry of chives, snipped with kitchen shears.

Charred Broccoli with Lemon & Parmesan Vinaigrette

Getting a nice hard sear on the vegetables that belong to the brassica family brings out the unique sweetness that they have to offer. There are many ways you can achieve this sear, but a scorching hot cast-iron pan is the best option.

FOR THE BROCCOLI

Salt and pepper, to taste

2 crowns of broccoli, quartered

3 tablespoons canola oil

½ cup Pickled Red Onion (see page 219), for garnish

½ cup toasted pine nuts, for garnish

FOR THE VINAIGRETTE

1 egg yolk

¼ cup grated Parmesan cheese

2 tablespoons fresh lemon juice

1 teaspoon Dijon mustard

1 cup canola oil

1. To begin preparations for the broccoli, bring water to a boil in a large saucepan and prepare an ice bath. Add salt until the water tastes like seawater (about 3 tablespoons of salt). Add the broccoli and cook for 1 minute. Remove the broccoli with a strainer and plunge it into the ice bath. Drain the broccoli and let it dry on a paper towel–lined plate.

2. To prepare the vinaigrette, place all of the ingredients, except for the canola oil, in a small bowl and stir to combine. While whisking continually, slowly stream in the canola oil until it has emulsified. Taste, adjust the seasoning as necessary, and set the vinaigrette aside.

3. Place the canola oil in a large cast-iron skillet and warm it over high heat. Lightly season the broccoli with salt and pepper and place it in the pan, taking care not to crowd the pan. Sear the broccoli until it is lightly charred on both sides.

4. Spread the vinaigrette over a serving dish, arrange the broccoli on top, garnish with the pickled onion and toasted pine nuts, and serve.

YIELD: 2 to 4 Servings / **ACTIVE TIME:** 30 Minutes / **TOTAL TIME:** 3 Hours

Jerk Chicken Wings

A marriage of Jamaican and Haitian flavors that elevates this accessible, irresistible appetizer.

FOR THE CHICKEN WINGS

2 lbs. chicken wings

¼ cup plus 1 tablespoon Jerk Spice Blend (see page 233)

2 cups all-purpose flour

Salt, to taste

Canola oil, as needed

FOR THE SAUCE

1 cup ketchup

1 tablespoon Jerk Spice Blend

1 teaspoon fresh lime juice

2 teaspoons Sos Ti Malice (see page 202)

2 teaspoons brown sugar

1. To begin preparations for the chicken wings, place the chicken in a bowl, add ¼ cup of the Jerk Spice Blend, and toss to combine. Place the chicken in the refrigerator and let it marinate for 2 hours.

2. Place the flour and remaining Jerk Spice Blend in a shallow bowl and stir to combine. Set the mixture aside.

3. Add canola oil to a cast-iron Dutch oven until it is about 2 inches deep and warm it to 325ºF.

4. Remove the chicken wings from the refrigerator and dredge them in the seasoned flour until they are completely coated.

5. Working in batches to avoid crowding the pot, gently slip the chicken wings into the hot oil. Fry until they are crispy and their interior temperature is 165ºF.

6. Transfer the fried chicken wings to a paper towel–lined plate and season them with salt.

7. To prepare the sauce, place all of the ingredients in a bowl and whisk until well combined.

8. Drizzle the sauce over the chicken wings or serve it alongside as a dipping sauce.

Smashed Potatoes with Summer Beans

Cast iron is a wonder at supplying contrasting textures, as these smashed potatoes, which carry the creamy interior of a boiled potato and the crispy exterior of French fries, exhibit.

1½ lbs. baby potatoes

Salt and pepper, to taste

5 garlic cloves, smashed

3 sprigs of fresh thyme

1 tablespoon black peppercorns

½ lb. summer beans, trimmed and cut into thirds

4 oz. pancetta, diced

Canola oil, as needed

½ cup grated Parmesan cheese

1. Rinse the potatoes under cold water and place them in a large pot. Cover them with water and add about 2 tablespoons of salt, the garlic, thyme, and peppercorns. Bring to a boil and then reduce the heat so that the water simmers. Cook until the potatoes are fork-tender, 15 to 20 minutes. Drain the potatoes and place them on paper towels to dry.

2. While the potatoes are cooking, bring water to a boil in a medium saucepan and prepare an ice bath. Add salt until the water tastes like seawater (about 3 tablespoons) and the beans and cook for 1 minute.

3. Drain the beans and plunge them into the ice bath. Drain the beans again, place them in a mixing bowl, and set them aside.

4. Place the pancetta in a small skillet and cook over medium-low heat, stirring occasionally, until the fat has rendered and the pancetta is crispy, about 6 minutes. Remove the pan from heat and set it aside.

5. Gently smash the potatoes to flatten them and pat them completely dry with paper towels.

6. Add the pancetta to the mixing bowl containing the beans.

7. Add canola oil to a large, deep cast-iron skillet until it is about ½ inch deep and warm it to 325°F. Working in batches to avoid crowding the pot, gently slip the smashed potatoes into the hot oil and fry on each side until the potatoes are golden brown, turning them as necessary.

8. Remove the lightly fried potatoes from the oil and add them to the mixing bowl. Season with salt and pepper, toss to combine, and transfer them to a serving dish.

9. Top the dish with the Parmesan and serve immediately.

YIELD: 2 Servings / **ACTIVE TIME:** 20 Minutes / **TOTAL TIME:** 30 Minutes

Caramelized Plums with Fennel, Orange, Ginger Yogurt & Pine Nuts

Plums are a wonderful fruit to work with, as they are great raw, roasted, or caramelized, and always look enticing on the plate.

1 cup champagne vinegar or white wine vinegar

½ cup fresh orange juice

3 tablespoons sugar, plus more as needed

½ teaspoon fine sea salt, plus more to taste

½ bulb of fennel, trimmed and shaved thin

2 tablespoons minced fresh ginger

½ cup Greek yogurt

2 tablespoons unsalted butter

3 ripe plums, halved and pitted

Fennel Pesto (see page 234)

1 Cara Cara orange, peeled and sliced, for garnish

1. Place the vinegar, orange juice, sugar, and salt in a small saucepan and bring to a boil. Place the shaved fennel in a mason jar and pour the hot brine over it. Cover the jar with plastic wrap and let the fennel pickle.

2. Place the ginger and yogurt in a bowl and stir to combine.

3. Place the butter in a large cast-iron skillet and melt it over medium heat. Place sugar in a shallow bowl and coat the cut sides of the plums with it. Place the plums in the pan, cut side down, and cook until they are caramelized.

4. Chop the plums and season them with salt. Place them in a bowl, add the pickled fennel, and toss to combine.

5. Spread the yogurt over the bottom of a serving dish.

6. Arrange the plums and pickled fennel on top, drizzle the Fennel Pesto over the salad, garnish with the orange, and serve.

Homemade Potato Chips

The key to making potato chips at home is running the thinly sliced potatoes under cold water, which removes some of the starch and prevents them from browning before they have a chance to become crispy in the hot oil. This seasoning blend is just to provide some direction—go with whatever flavors you find appealing, as even a standard combination of salt and pepper is great on a crispy chip.

Canola oil, as needed

2 medium Idaho potatoes

2 medium sweet potatoes

2 teaspoons paprika

1 teaspoon vinegar powder

2 tablespoons fine sea salt

1 tablespoon black pepper

1. Add canola oil to a cast-iron Dutch oven until it is about 2 inches deep and warm it to 300°F.

2. Using a mandoline, cut the potatoes into thin rounds and place them in a container. Cut the sweet potatoes into thin rounds and place them in a separate container.

3. Rinse the potatoes and sweet potatoes under cold water.

4. Place the paprika, vinegar powder, salt, and pepper in a small bowl, stir to combine, and set the mixture aside.

5. Drain the potatoes and sweet potatoes and pat them dry with paper towels.

6. Working in batches to avoid crowding the pot, gently slip the potatoes into the pot and fry until they are crispy and golden brown. Repeat with the sweet potatoes.

7. As the potato and sweet potato chips finish cooking, use a slotted spoon to transfer them to a mixing bowl lined with paper towels. Season them with the spice mixture, toss to combine, and transfer them to a serving bowl. Serve once all of the chips have been cooked and seasoned.

YIELD: 4 Servings / **ACTIVE TIME:** 30 Minutes / **TOTAL TIME:** 45 Minutes

Crispy Brussels Sprouts with Maple & Cider Vinaigrette

Brussels sprouts are something of a controversial ingredient, as some love them, and others positively hate them. We would argue that many in that latter group just haven't had them prepared correctly yet. This recipe is certain to remedy that.

FOR THE BRUSSELS SPROUTS

½ cup diced pancetta

Canola oil, as needed

1 lb. Brussels sprouts, trimmed and halved

½ cup toasted pistachios

Salt and pepper, to taste

½ cup goat cheese, crumbled

1 apple, cored and sliced

FOR THE VINAIGRETTE

2 tablespoons apple cider vinegar

2 tablespoons apple cider

1 tablespoon maple syrup

1 teaspoon fine sea salt, plus more to taste

1½ teaspoons Dijon mustard

Black pepper, to taste

¾ cup canola oil

1. To begin preparations for the Brussels sprouts, place the pancetta in a large skillet and cook it over medium heat until its fat has rendered and it is golden brown, 4 to 6 minutes. Remove the pancetta from the pan and set it aside.

2. Add canola oil to a cast-iron Dutch oven until it is about 2 inches deep and warm it to 350°F.

3. To prepare the vinaigrette, place all of the ingredients, except for the canola oil, in a small mixing bowl and whisk to combine. While whisking continually, add the canola oil until it has emulsified. Season the vinaigrette with salt and pepper and set it aside.

4. Gently slip the Brussels sprouts into the hot oil and fry until they are crispy and golden brown, 6 to 8 minutes.

5. Transfer the fried Brussels sprouts to a paper towel–lined plate and let them drain.

6. Place the Brussels sprouts in a bowl, add the vinaigrette, pancetta, and pistachios, season with salt and pepper, and toss to combine.

7. Top with the goat cheese and apple and serve.

Socca

Residing somewhere between a flatbread and a pancake, this delectable appetizer is beloved in Southern France.

---

7 tablespoons extra-virgin olive oil

3 small onions, chopped

1½ cups chickpea flour

½ teaspoon kosher salt, plus more to taste

1 teaspoon turmeric

1½ cups water

Black pepper, to taste

2 tablespoons chopped fresh chives

Tzatziki (see page 235), for serving

1. Place 1 tablespoon of the olive oil in a small cast-iron skillet and warm it over medium-high heat. Add the onions, reduce the heat to low, and cook, stirring occasionally, until the onions are caramelized, about 30 minutes. Transfer the onions to a bowl and let them cool.

2. Place the chickpea flour, salt, turmeric, and water in a mixing bowl and whisk to combine. While whisking, slowly drizzle in 2 tablespoons of the olive oil. When the mixture comes together as a smooth batter, season it with salt and pepper.

3. Warm the cast-iron pan over medium-high heat. Add 1 tablespoon of the olive oil and then add ⅓ cup of the batter, tilting the pan to make sure the batter is evenly distributed. Reduce the heat to medium and cook until the batter starts to firm up, about 2 minutes.

4. Sprinkle some of the caramelized onions over the socca and cook until the edges are golden brown, 2 to 4 minutes. Flip the socca over and cook until it is golden brown and cooked through, about 2 minutes.

5. Gently remove the socca from the pan and repeat Steps 3 and 4 until all of the batter and caramelized onions have been used.

6. When all of the socca have been made, sprinkle the chives over the top and serve with Tzatziki.

Lamb Heart Kalbi in Lettuce Wraps

Don't tell your guest just what they're eating until they ask you what these bits of deliciousness are. To really impress, serve these with a glass of sparkling Rosé.

¾ cup chopped onion

¾ cup soy sauce

¼ cup sesame oil

2 tablespoons sugar

2 tablespoons brown sugar

2 tablespoons mirin (sweet rice wine)

3 garlic cloves

A small knob of fresh ginger, peeled and sliced

1 tablespoon toasted sesame seeds

1½ teaspoons red pepper flakes

6 lamb hearts

2 tablespoons corn oil

12 romaine lettuce spears, taken from the inside of the head

12 slices of jalapeño pepper, for garnish

Fresh cilantro, chopped, for garnish

1. Place the onion, soy sauce, sesame oil, sugar, brown sugar, mirin, garlic, and ginger in a blender and blend on high for 1 minute. Transfer the mixture to a medium glass bowl and stir in the sesame seeds and red pepper flakes.

2. Trim off some but not all the fat from the surface of the lamb hearts. Cut the hearts in half and lay the cut sides up on a cutting board. Trim some of the veins and arteries from the inside of the hearts. Rinse the hearts under cold running water, add them to the marinade, and marinate in the refrigerator for 30 minutes.

3. Remove the hearts from the marinade and pat them dry on paper towels. Heat a large cast-iron skillet over high heat until hot. Add 1 tablespoon of corn oil and carefully add half the lamb hearts to the pan. Sear very quickly, about 1 minute on each side, until the outside is blackened and caramelized, but the inside is still rare. Remove from the heat, then heat the remaining tablespoon of oil and sear the remaining lamb hearts.

4. Place a piece of lamb heart on each romaine lettuce spear and garnish with a slice of jalapeño and chopped cilantro. Serve immediately.

YIELD: 2 Servings / **ACTIVE TIME:** 20 Minutes / **TOTAL TIME:** 45 Minutes

Roasted & Stuffed Sardines

Sardines are easier to prepare whole than most fish, as their bones are edible, and full of nutrients.

5 whole, fresh sardines

3 tablespoons extra-virgin olive oil

½ white onion, chopped

¼ cup chopped celery

1 teaspoon kosher salt

1 tablespoon paprika

Pinch of cumin

2 garlic cloves, minced

2 tablespoons water

¼ cup chopped fresh parsley

1 cup day-old bread pieces

Tahini & Yogurt Sauce (see page 201), for serving

1. Clean the sardines: make an incision in the belly of each one from head to tail. Remove the guts and carefully snap the spines at the neck and tail. This will leave the sardines intact enough to hold their shape when roasted. Rinse the sardines and set them aside.

2. Place 2 tablespoons of the olive oil in a medium cast-iron skillet and warm it over medium-high heat. Add the onion, celery, salt, paprika, cumin, and garlic and cook, stirring frequently, until the onion is translucent, about 3 minutes.

3. Add the water and simmer for 3 or 4 minutes. Add the parsley and bread and cook, stirring frequently, allowing the bread to absorb the liquid and brown a bit. After 5 minutes, remove the pan from heat.

4. Preheat the oven to 450°F.

5. Place the sardines in a large cast-iron skillet, keeping them nestled against each other so they hold their shape better. Fill the sardines' bellies with the stuffing, drizzle the remaining olive oil over them, and place the pan in the oven.

6. Roast the stuffed sardines until they reach an internal temperature of 145°F, 15 to 20 minutes.

7. Remove the sardines from the oven and serve with the tahini sauce.

Roasted & Stuffed Sardines
see page 39

Couscous Arancini

This recipe is a great way to use up leftover couscous, and provide your loved ones with a massively comforting dish.

---

2 cups couscous

1 tablespoon paprika

1 tablespoon garlic powder

2 teaspoons kosher salt

1 teaspoon cumin

1 cup crumbled feta cheese

Canola oil, as needed

1. Place 2½ cups water in a saucepan and bring it to a boil.

2. Place the couscous and the seasonings in a mixing bowl and stir until well combined. Add the boiling water to the couscous and cover the bowl with plastic wrap. After 10 minutes, use a fork to fluff the couscous.

3. Add ½ cup of feta to the couscous and stir to incorporate it.

4. Add canola oil to a cast-iron Dutch oven until it is about 2 inches deep and warm it to 350°F.

5. Using your hands, form 1 oz. portions of the couscous into balls. Press into each ball with your thumb and make a depression. Fill this with some of the remaining feta and then close the ball over it.

6. Working in batches of 4 to avoid crowding the pot, gently slip the balls into the hot oil and fry until they are golden brown, about 4 minutes. Transfer the fried arancini to a paper towel–lined plate to drain and cool and enjoy once all of them have been cooked.

YIELD: 4 Servings / **ACTIVE TIME:** 30 Minutes / **TOTAL TIME:** 45 Minutes

Taquitos de Papa

Simple and classic homestyle cooking, taquitos are a perfect way to add an intriguing, light, and delicious appetizer to your next gathering.

2 russet potatoes, peeled and quartered

Salt, to taste

2 large tomatoes, finely diced

½ onion, finely diced

2 jalapeño chile peppers, stems and seeds removed, chopped

1 cup fresh cilantro, chopped

2 cups shredded green cabbage

2 cups crumpled cotija cheese

12 Corn Tortillas (see page 214)

1 cup extra-virgin olive oil

1. Place the potatoes in a small saucepan and cover with cold water. Bring it to a boil, season the water with salt, and reduce the heat so that the potatoes simmer. Cook until tender, about 18 minutes.

2. Drain the potatoes, place them in a mixing bowl, and mash until smooth. Season with salt, add the remaining ingredients, except for the tortillas and olive oil, and stir to combine.

3. Fill the tortillas with the potato mixture and either roll them up tight or fold over to form half-moons.

4. Place the olive oil in a deep cast-iron skillet and warm it over medium heat. Gently slip the filled tortillas into the hot oil and fry until they are browned and crispy.

5. Place the taquitos on a paper towel–lined plate and let them drain and cool slightly before serving.

Taquitos de Papa
see page 43

Fried Cabbage

Sean Brock: "Where I'm from, fried doesn't always mean deep-fried, like French fries. Most of the time, in fact, it means skillet-fried. The trick with this recipe is to start with high heat so you caramelize the bottom layer of cabbage while the rest of the cabbage, stacked on top, releases its juices. Don't cook the cabbage to death; it should still have a little bite. Try this technique with potatoes or turnips too. You won't be disappointed."

2 tablespoons lard

1 tablespoon rendered bacon fat

½ medium head green cabbage (about 1 lb.), tough outer leaves discarded, cored and cut into 1-inch chunks

1½ teaspoons kosher salt

2 teaspoons honey vinegar

¼ teaspoon hot sauce

1 teaspoon fresh lemon juice

1. Heat the lard and bacon fat in a large cast-iron skillet over high heat until just starting to smoke. Add one-third of the cabbage, season with ½ teaspoon of salt, and cook, undisturbed, for about 1 minute to begin to caramelize the cabbage.

2. Stir, add another one-third of the cabbage, season with another ½ teaspoon of the salt, and cook, stirring occasionally, for a minute or so, until the cabbage has decreased slightly in volume. Add the remaining cabbage and ½ teaspoon salt and cook, stirring, for 1 minute.

3. Reduce the heat to medium, cover, and cook until the cabbage is just tender and starting to break down, 4 to 5 minutes.

4. Remove the cabbage from the stove and stir in the vinegar, hot sauce, and lemon juice. Serve straight from the skillet.

Concia

Both earthy and refreshing, concia is the perfect accompaniment to a heavier meal.

---

3 zucchini, sliced lengthwise into ¼-inch-thick pieces

Salt and pepper, to taste

Avocado oil, as needed

6 garlic cloves, minced

½ bunch of fresh basil, chopped

¼ cup white wine vinegar

1. Season the zucchini slices with salt and pepper on both sides, place them on a paper towel–lined baking sheet, and let them rest for 10 minutes.

2. Pat the zucchini dry and replace the paper towels on the baking sheet. Add avocado oil to a large, deep cast-iron skillet until it is ½ inch deep and warm it over medium heat. Working in batches of 6 slices, gently slip the zucchini into the hot oil, making sure that the pieces all lie flat and do not overlap. Fry the zucchini until golden brown all over, about 5 minutes, turning as necessary. Transfer the fried zucchini to the paper towel–lined baking sheet and let it drain.

3. Place all of the fried zucchini in a mixing bowl. Season it with salt and pepper, add the garlic, basil, and vinegar, and gently stir until the zucchini is evenly coated.

4. Cover the bowl with plastic wrap and chill it in the refrigerator for 5 hours before enjoying. To serve, let the concia come to room temperature.

YIELD: 4 Servings / **ACTIVE TIME:** 10 Minutes / **TOTAL TIME:** 30 Minutes

Smoky Seared Eggplant

A simple but refined and flavorful way to prepare eggplant.

---

1 cup wood chips

1 onion, quartered

2 teaspoons kosher salt

¼ cup avocado oil

1 small eggplant, trimmed and cubed

1 red bell pepper, stem and seeds removed, diced

¼ cup balsamic vinegar

1. Place the wood chips in a small cast-iron skillet and light them on fire. Place the cast-iron pan into a roasting pan and place the onion beside the skillet. Cover the roasting pan with aluminum foil and smoke the onion for 20 minutes.

2. Transfer the onion to a food processor and puree until smooth. Add 1 teaspoon of the salt, stir to combine, and set the puree aside.

3. Place the avocado oil in a large cast-iron skillet and warm it over high heat. Add the eggplant, season it with the remaining salt, and sear it for 1 minute. Turn the eggplant over, add the bell pepper, and cook for another minute.

4. Add the balsamic vinegar and toss to coat.

5. To serve, spoon the onion puree onto the serving plates and top with the vegetables.

Smoky Seared Eggplant
see page 49

FOR THE PEPPERS

2 tablespoons extra-virgin olive oil

2 garlic cloves, sliced paper thin

½ cup thinly sliced sweet onion

3 red bell peppers (about 6 oz. each), cored and thinly sliced

¼ cup apple cider vinegar

1 tablespoon light brown sugar

1 cup Chicken Stock (see page 212)

2 teaspoons kosher salt

½ teaspoon freshly ground black pepper

FOR THE GRILLED BREAD

12-inch piece of baguette

2 tablespoons extra-virgin olive oil

Kosher salt and freshly ground black pepper, to taste

FOR THE CLAMS

8 oz. smoked breakfast sausage

1 cup canned whole tomatoes, roughly chopped, with their juices

¼ cup heavy cream

¼ cup dry white wine

1 bay leaf

32 littleneck clams, scrubbed under cold running water

1 tablespoon fresh lemon juice

1 tablespoon hot sauce

Fresh herbs, chopped, for garnish

YIELD: 4 Servings / **ACTIVE TIME:** 30 Minutes / **TOTAL TIME:** 1 Hour

Clams with Sausage, Braised Peppers & Grilled Bread

Sean Brock: "When I make this dish, I use my backyard wood-burning oven to cook the clams and impart an incredible smoky flavor to the sauce. You can easily re-create it at home on the grill. The combination of sausage and braised peppers is delicious, and when the clams open and give up their juices, it goes to the next level."

1. For the braised peppers: Heat the olive oil in a large skillet over medium-high heat until it shimmers. Add the garlic and onion and cook, stirring frequently, until translucent and softened, about 3 minutes. Add the bell peppers and cook, stirring frequently, until they begin to soften, about 4 minutes. Stir in the vinegar and brown sugar and cook, stirring occasionally, until the vinegar has almost completely evaporated, about 10 minutes. Add the stock and cook, stirring occasionally, until the stock has reduced to about ¼ cup and the peppers are very soft, about 30 minutes. Season with the salt and black pepper, remove from the stove, and set aside.

2. For the grilled bread: Prepare a hot fire in a charcoal grill, removing the grill rack and distributing the hot coal in an even layer in the bottom of the grill. Place the grill rack at its normal height.

3. Cut the baguette crosswise in half. Cut each piece lengthwise in half and then lengthwise in half again, producing eight 6-inch-long pieces of bread. Lightly brush the wedges of bread with the olive oil and season lightly with salt and pepper. Grill the bread cut side down until lightly charred and toasted, about 4 minutes. Remove from the grill and set aside.

4. For the clams: Cook the sausage in a large cast-iron skillet set on top of the grill rack, stirring frequently, until browned and broken up into small pieces. Add the tomatoes, braised peppers, cream, wine, and bay leaf and cook until the mixture has slightly reduced and thickened, about 10 minutes. Add the clams, put the lid on the grill, and cook until the clams have opened, about 5 minutes. Remove and discard the bay leaf.

5. To serve: Divide the clams, peppers, and sausage among four warm rimmed soup plates. Drizzle each portion with the lemon juice and hot sauce, sprinkle fresh herbs over the top, and place 2 pieces of grilled bread on the rim of each soup plate.

YIELD: 6 Servings / **ACTIVE TIME:** 30 Minutes / **TOTAL TIME:** 1 Hour and 30 Minutes

Fried Green Tomatoes

Sean Brock: "There are a hundred different ways to make fried green tomatoes, and some are more successful than others. The problem with most bad fried green tomatoes is overbreading, which can muffle the character and flavor of the tomatoes. I soak the sliced tomatoes in seasoned buttermilk and give them a dredge in cornmeal, but the most important part of the recipe is letting the breaded tomatoes rest in the refrigerator before you fry them. That rest eliminates the need for additional flour and a messy egg wash, and the tomatoes can be breaded up to 2 hours ahead of time, which is convenient when you're entertaining."

1½ cups full-fat buttermilk

1 teaspoon hot sauce

1 tablespoon plus 1 teaspoon kosher salt, plus more to taste

1½ lbs. medium green tomatoes, cored and cut into ½-inch-thick slices

1½ cups fine yellow cornmeal

½ cup all-purpose flour

½ teaspoon freshly ground black pepper

½ cup canola oil

¼ cup lard

1. Combine the buttermilk, hot sauce, and 1 teaspoon of the salt in a large bowl. Add the green tomato slices and toss them to coat. Let marinate at room temperature for 30 minutes, occasionally turning the tomatoes to ensure even coating.

2. Line a rimmed baking sheet with parchment paper. Combine the cornmeal, flour, the remaining tablespoon of salt, and the pepper in a shallow baking dish. Working with one slice at a time, shake off any excess buttermilk from the tomatoes, dredge in the cornmeal mixture, shake off any excess, and transfer to the prepared baking sheet. Transfer the baking sheet to the refrigerator and let the slices rest for at least 30 minutes and up to 2 hours.

3. Fifteen minutes before frying, remove the tomatoes from the refrigerator. Preheat the oven to 200°F. Line a rimmed baking sheet with paper towels. Combine the canola oil and lard in a large, deep cast-iron skillet and heat over medium heat to 350°F.

4. Working in batches, without crowding the pan, fry the tomatoes until crispy and golden brown on both sides, about 4 minutes; using a fork, carefully turn the tomatoes over halfway through frying to ensure that they cook evenly. As they are done, transfer the tomatoes to the prepared baking sheet, season lightly with salt, and keep warm in the oven while you fry the remaining slices. Arrange the fried green tomatoes on a serving plate and serve.

YIELD: 4 Servings / **ACTIVE TIME:** 15 Minutes / **TOTAL TIME:** 25 Minutes

Fried Bologna with Pickled Peach Mustard

Sean Brock: "Like many kids in the South, I grew up eating fried bologna. It was one of the first things I was trusted to cook by myself. I loved getting out my mom's cast-iron skillet and cutting four slits in the edges of the bologna slice so it wouldn't curl up. The smell of it frying up always reminds me how lucky I am to have been raised in the Appalachian Mountains."

FOR THE MUSTARD

½ cup Dijon mustard

½ cup drained Pickled Peaches (see page 244), plus 1 teaspoon of their pickling juice

¾ teaspoon kosher salt

FOR THE BOLOGNA

1½ lbs. high-quality bologna, cut into 12 slices

2 tablespoons unsalted butter

1. For the mustard: Combine the mustard, pickled peaches, pickling juice, and salt in a blender and blend on high until completely smooth, about 1 minute. Transfer to a small serving dish. (The mustard can be made ahead. Tightly covered, it will keep for up to 2 weeks in the refrigerator.)

2. For the bologna: Line a baking sheet with paper towels. Using a paring knife, notch each slice of bologna four times evenly around its circumference, cutting about ½ inch into the bologna.

3. Heat 1 tablespoon of the butter in a large cast-iron skillet over medium-high heat until foamy. Add half the bologna slices in a single layer and cook until deep brown on the first side, about 1½ minutes. Flip the slices and cook until the other side is deep brown, about 1 minute more. Transfer the fried bologna to the prepared baking sheet. Wipe out the skillet, add the remaining tablespoon of butter, and cook the remaining bologna slices.

4. To serve: Arrange the bologna slices on a platter with the pickled peach mustard.

Fresh Flageolets with Braised Baby Leeks & Chanterelle Mushrooms

According to Gabrielle Hamilton, the key to this dish is making sure "that your leeks are fully cooked. Make sure there is no raw bite at the center and no 'al dente' texture."

1 lb. shelled fresh flageolets

10 baby leeks

1 lb. chanterelle mushrooms

8 cups Chicken Stock (see page 212)

3 garlic cloves

1 cup loosely packed parsley leaves

2 medium shallots

Unsalted butter, as needed

Salt and pepper, to taste

Extra-virgin olive oil, as needed

1. Simmer the flageolets in water seasoned with just salt, bay leaf, and a few black peppercorns. Fresh beans are a different game—they will only need 30 minutes, approximately, to lose their raw quality and start to show their true waxy nature. Strain when cooked.

2. Clean baby leeks but leave them whole. Clean chanterelles with a few brisk dunks in a sink full of cold water. Chop garlic. Chop parsley. Slice shallots into thin rings.

3. In mixed fats, sauté the chanterelles over medium-high heat in a cast-iron skillet; season with salt and pepper.

4. When the water they release starts to reduce and have body; add a little more fat and the chopped garlic and reduce the flame just a tad.

5. Let the garlic soften but not take on any color.

6. Push the mushrooms into a ring at the edge, clearing space in the center of the pan.

7. Lay in the leeks in one layer and sweat them until their exteriors are bright green and turning translucent; roll them around a bit; season briefly with salt during the sweating. You want to take the hard raw edge off of them and let some of their sweetness start to develop before adding the stock to fully braise them.

8. Scatter the parcooked flagelots generously in and around the pan, to create a more or less equal ratio of beans to leeks and mushrooms.

9. Ladle in stock to not quite cover but to flood the contents.

10. Season with salt and pepper to taste, and bring to a gentle simmer.

11. Lay the handle of your wooden spoon across the pan with the bowl of the spoon resting beyond the lip, and set a lid down on the pan to loosely cover during the simmer. The spoon handle gives a better hap to allow steam to escape than just setting the lid askew. We want the weak watery condensation to escape but the stock and the sweet, earthy juices of the leeks and mushrooms to continue to commingle and reduce together.

12. Stir in chopped parsley and one nut of cold butter before plating.

Spoonbread with Kale & Bacon

Edward Lee: "As the name suggests, this dish is best eaten with a spoon, and you've got to eat it while it is piping hot. Spoonbread is somewhere between a bread and a custard, and it's one of those recipes that demands a well-seasoned cast-iron skillet. It just won't work without one. And you'll get better results making spoonbread in a few 6-inch cast-iron skillets than one large one."

8 oz. bacon, diced

⅓ cup chopped onion

4 oz. kale, cleaned, stemmed, and coarsely chopped

3 cups whole milk

1¼ cups white cornmeal

3 large eggs, beaten

2 tablespoons unsalted butter, melted, plus more for the skillets

1¾ teaspoons baking powder

1 teaspoon kosher salt

1. Heat a large cast-iron skillet over medium-high heat and add the bacon. Cook for 2 minutes, until the fat is beginning to render and the bacon is lightly crisped, then add the onions and sauté for 3 minutes, or until the onions are soft. Add the kale and sauté for 10 minutes, or until the kale is tender. Remove from the heat and set aside.

2. Preheat the oven to 400°F.

3. Bring the milk to a gentle boil in a small pot over medium heat. Stir the cornmeal into the boiling milk and cook, stirring constantly, until thick, 3 to 4 minutes. Remove from the heat, transfer to a bowl, and allow to cool.

4. Add the eggs, butter, baking powder, and salt to the cornmeal and beat with a hand mixer on medium speed for 6 minutes, until all the ingredients are thoroughly mixed together and the eggs have stiffened the batter slightly. Fold in the bacon and kale.

5. Heat a teaspoon of butter in each of three 6-inch cast-iron skillets over high for 2 minutes, or until the butter foams. Pour the batter into the hot skillet(s), transfer to the oven, and bake for 15 to 18 minutes. Serve the spoonbread in the pans hot from the oven.

YIELD: *4 Servings* / **ACTIVE TIME:** 10 Minutes / **TOTAL TIME:** 25 Minutes

Tequila Cheese Dip

A show-stopping preparation that will deliver on the expectations that build as you carry it to the table.

___

6 oz. Oaxaca cheese, cubed

½ plum tomato, diced

¼ white onion, diced

2 tablespoons diced green chile peppers

2 tablespoons sugar

¼ cup fresh lime juice

1 teaspoon chili powder

1 oz. tequila

1. Preheat the oven to 350ºF. Place the cheese, tomato, onion, and chiles in a small cast-iron skillet and stir to combine. Set the mixture aside.

2. Combine the sugar, lime juice, and chili powder in a small saucepan and cook over medium heat, stirring to dissolve the sugar, until the mixture is syrupy.

3. Drizzle the syrup over the cheese mixture, place it in the oven, and bake until the cheese has melted and is golden brown on top, about 15 minutes.

4. Remove the pan from the oven, pour the tequila over the mixture, and use a long match or a wand lighter to ignite it. Bring the flaming skillet to the table and enjoy once the flames have gone out.

Glazed Okra

When you are shopping, try to avoid any okra that have brown spots, as they indicate it has been sitting for a while.

---

2 tablespoons extra-virgin olive oil

12 okra pods

1 teaspoon kosher salt

1 teaspoon black pepper

1 teaspoon brown sugar

1 teaspoon white vinegar

Sweet Potato Puree (see page 203)

¼ cup crumbled goat cheese

1. Place the olive oil in a large cast-iron skillet and warm it over high heat. Add the okra, season it with the salt and pepper, and cook until the okra is browned all over, turning it as necessary.

2. Remove the okra from the pan and set it aside. Turn off the heat but leave the pan on the stove.

3. Place the brown sugar and vinegar in the pan and stir until the mixture is syrupy.

4. Spread the Sweet Potato Puree on a serving plate and arrange the okra in a line on top of it. Sprinkle the goat cheese over the dish, drizzle the glaze over the top, and enjoy.

YIELD: 4 Servings / ACTIVE TIME: 20 Minutes / TOTAL TIME: 35 Minutes

Potatoes & Ramps Cooked in Ham Fat

Sean Brock: "After a spring day of ramp hunting with chef David Chang and me, legendary curemaster Allan Benton pulled his car off the road on the creek side and set up a camp kitchen. He pulled out a cast-iron skillet, some of his famous ham and bacon, a sack of potatoes, black walnut brownies, and a plate of cornbread his wife, Sharon, had sent us out with. Dave and I washed the ramps in the creek while Allan tended the fire. He fried up the ham and bacon, added the potatoes and ramps, covered the skillet, and cooked up some of the best food I've ever eaten. This plate of food is my homage to that meal. Serve this dish in the spring, when ramps are in season, and thank Mr. Benton."

---

1 cup rendered ham fat

1 lb. small Butterball potatoes (about ½ inch wide and 2 inches long) or new potatoes, cut into ½-inch-thick slices

8 oz. ramps, cleaned, dried, and hairy root ends removed

1 tablespoon fresh lemon juice

Kosher salt and freshly ground black pepper, to taste

¼ cup sliced Pickled Ramps (see page 204)

1. Melt the ham fat over medium heat in a deep saucepan just large enough to hold the potatoes in a loose single layer. Add the potatoes (they should be submerged in the fat) and cook until a knife inserted in a potato meets no resistance, about 15 minutes. Remove from the stove and let the potatoes cool in the fat.

2. Heat a large cast-iron skillet over medium-high heat. Spoon 2 table-spoons of ham fat from the potatoes into the skillet, add the potatoes in a single layer, and cook until golden brown on the bottom and starting to crisp, about 2 minutes. Turn the potatoes over and cook until the other side is golden brown and starting to crisp, about 2 minutes. Add the fresh ramps to the skillet, cover, and cook until just wilted, 2 to 3 minutes. Uncover, add the lemon juice, and season liberally with salt and pepper.

3. Transfer to a serving bowl, sprinkle with the Pickled Ramps and serve.

Glazed Okra
see page 62

Beets with Walnut Dukkah

Dukkah is a nut-and-seed blend that, in Egypt, is often eaten in the same way that contemporary Americans consume trail mix. Using its crunch to add a contrasting texture to this dish makes for a unique preparation.

---

2 large beets, unpeeled

Pinch of kosher salt

2 tablespoons chopped walnuts

2 tablespoons chopped hazelnuts

2 teaspoons black pepper

2 teaspoons poppy seeds

2 teaspoons black sesame seeds

1 tablespoon avocado oil

¼ cup Labneh (see page 205)

1 cinnamon stick

1. Place the beets and salt in a saucepan with at least 5 cups of water and bring to a boil. Cook the beets until a knife can easily pass through them, 30 to 40 minutes.

2. Drain the beets, run them under cold water, and peel off the skins and stems; it is easiest to do this while the beets are still hot.

3. Cut the peeled beets into ¾-inch cubes and set them aside.

4. Place the nuts in a resealable bag and use a rolling pin to crush them. Transfer to a small bowl, add the black pepper and seeds, and stir to combine. Set the mixture aside.

5. Place the avocado oil in a large cast-iron skillet and warm it over high heat. Place the beets in the pan and sear until well browned all over, about 5 minutes, turning the beets as necessary. Transfer the beets to a paper towel–lined plate to drain.

6. To serve, spread the Labneh across a shallow bowl, pile the beets on top, and sprinkle the dukkah over the dish. Grate the cinnamon stick over the beets until the dish is to your taste and enjoy.

Nori Crackers

Nori is a dried edible seaweed that crisps up beautifully when fried, as you'll see as soon as you make these crackers.

1 egg

1 tablespoon water

3 spring roll wrappers

3 sheets of nori

6 tablespoons sesame seeds

Canola oil, as needed

Salt, to taste

1. Combine the egg and water and brush the spring roll wrappers with the egg wash. Place a sheet of nori on top of each wrapper and brush the nori with the egg wash. Sprinkle the sesame seeds on top and let them sit for 10 minutes.

2. Add canola oil to a cast-iron Dutch oven until it is about 2 inches deep and warm it to 300ºF. Cut each sheet into nine squares, place them in the oil, and fry until browned and crispy, about 5 minutes. Transfer to a paper towel–lined plate, season with salt, and enjoy.

YIELD: 4 Servings / ACTIVE TIME: 25 Minutes / TOTAL TIME: 1 Hour

Soft-Cooked Zucchini with Green Onion and Poblanos

A recipe made for the surplus of zucchini that arrives every summer.

1½ lbs. firm, tightly pored, and shiny green zucchini

¼ lb. new green onions or scallions

3 garlic cloves

1 small glossy, firm poblano chile pepper

½ cup unsalted butter

Salt, to taste

1. Wash zucchini well under cold running water and wipe dry and thoroughly with a clean kitchen towel. Cut the zucchini into ¾-inch disks, and include the delicious and tender stems at the tops that attach the fruit to the vine (but shave off the dry and discolored tips).

2. Wash the scallions or green onions thoroughly in a cold-water bath, letting the dirt and sand settle down to the bottom of the sink. Wash multiple times if necessary. Trim the roots if they have browned and look old and unappealing, but if we are lucky enough to have fresh and vital roots still attached, leave them on, making sure they are free of sand.

3. Cut the scallions/green onions into ¼-inch rings, cutting as far up into the green of the stalk as you possibly can. In some cases, you can get 100 percent yield from the onion, but others get a little too fibrous and unappetizingly hollow at the very tip. Trim according to the condition of the onion in front of you.

4. Peel the garlic, trim the hard dry tips, and cut across the grain into thin slices.

5. In a heavy enameled cast-iron Dutch oven, melt one-third of the butter over gentle heat.

6. Add onions, pepper, and garlic, season with salt, and let sweat 2 to 3 minutes, with the lid on, letting the accumulating steam run back into the pot.

7. Add the zucchini and season again with salt to taste. Add another knob of butter. Stir well to coat the zucchini and sweat briefly.

8. Add the remaining butter and cover with a tight-fitting lid. Allow the dish to braise in its own liquid approximately 20 to 25 minutes, until soft and nearly falling apart.

Chicharron en Salsa Roja

Should you be in the mood for something sweet rather than spicy, swap out the salsa for some chocolate ganache.

1 lb. pork belly, cut into 1-inch-wide and 6-inch-long strips

1½ tablespoons kosher salt

4 cups lard or canola oil

4 large tomatoes

3 serrano chile peppers

3 garlic cloves

Corn Tortillas (see page 214), warmed, for serving

1. Set a wire rack in a rimmed baking sheet. Season the pork belly with the salt.

2. Place the lard in a cast-iron Dutch oven (make sure it doesn't reach more than halfway up the sides of the pot) and warm it over medium-high heat. Add the pork belly and cook until golden brown and very crispy, about 1 hour.

3. Place the pork belly on the wire rack and let it drain. When the pork is cool enough to handle, chop it into ½-inch pieces.

4. Fill a medium saucepan with water and bring it to a boil. Add the tomatoes, serrano peppers, and garlic and cook until tender, about 10 minutes. Drain, transfer the vegetables to a blender, and puree until smooth.

5. Return the puree to the saucepan, add the pork belly, and simmer for about 20 minutes, so that the chicharron absorbs some of the sauce. Serve with tortillas and enjoy.

YIELD: 6 Servings / ACTIVE TIME: 30 Minutes / TOTAL TIME: 30 Minutes

Glazed Spam Musubi

A recipe that proves Spam gets a bad rap. If you don't have a musubi mold, use the Spam can to mold the rice blocks, making sure to rinse it out first.

---

2 tablespoons soy sauce

2 tablespoons brown sugar

½ teaspoon mirin

2 teaspoons avocado oil

1 can of Spam, sliced horizontally into 8 pieces

6 cups cooked short-grain white rice, at room temperature

3 sheets of roasted nori, cut into thirds

2 teaspoons furikake seasoning

1. Place the soy sauce, brown sugar, and mirin in a bowl and whisk until the sugar has dissolved. Set the glaze aside.

2. Place the avocado oil in a large cast-iron skillet and warm it over medium-high heat. Add the Spam and cook until it is browned and crispy on each side, 4 to 6 minutes.

3. Pour the glaze over the Spam and turn off the heat. Let the Spam sit for 1 minute, then turn it in the glaze until it is evenly coated. Transfer the glazed Spam to a plate and set it aside.

4. Fill a musubi mold with some of the cooked rice and press down to pack it tightly. Remove the formed block of rice from the mold and repeat until all of the rice has been molded.

5. Place the nori on the counter, shiny side down. Place a piece of Spam in the center of each piece and sprinkle the furikake over the Spam. Place one of the molded rice blocks atop the Spam, carefully wrap the nori over the rice, and enjoy immediately.

YIELD: 4 Servings / ACTIVE TIME: 15 Minutes / TOTAL TIME: 30 Minutes

Warm Mushroom Toast with Port, Herbs & Ricotta

Erin French: "This dish came about when one of my mushroom guys turned up with baskets and baskets of different types of mushrooms. I thought back to one of my favorite ways to eat them: buttered and sautéed in port, reminiscent of my dad's campfire version from our days camping up at Mount Katahdin. Then I spooned them over a schmear of ricotta cheese on toasted sourdough, and layered in the damp, mossy taste of woods with a whisper of thyme and rosemary."

---

2 tablespoons extra-virgin olive oil, plus more for drizzling

½ lb. mixed mushrooms (such as cremini, shiitake, and button)

2 sprigs of fresh thyme

1 sprig of fresh rosemary

Salt and pepper, to taste

¼ cup Port

3 tablespoons unsalted butter

4 thick slices of good sourdough bread

1 garlic clove

½ cup ricotta cheese

1 small handful of arugula

¼ cup shaved pecorino cheese

1. Preheat the oven to 425°F.

2. Set a large cast-iron skillet over high heat and pour in the olive oil. Add the mushrooms, thyme, and rosemary. Season with a good pinch of salt and a few twists of pepper. Sauté for 1 minute.

3. Add the Port and bring to a boil. Cook for a minute, then add the butter and transfer the pan to the oven. Roast until the mushrooms are just tender, 5 minutes.

4. Meanwhile, drizzle the bread with a little olive oil and crisp it up in the oven (or on a hot grill or in a toaster). When just golden and crisp, about 4 minutes, rub the toast with the garlic clove.

5. Top each piece of bread with a schmear of ricotta, a few leaves of arugula, and mushrooms and a bit of pan juice. Sprinkle with pecorino and serve.

Baozi

Searing the baozi after they steam is the key to taking them to the next level.

---

10 oz. ground pork

1 tablespoon minced fresh ginger

⅓ cup chopped scallions

¼ teaspoon kosher salt

⅛ teaspoon white pepper

1 teaspoon sugar

1 tablespoon plus 1 teaspoon soy sauce

2 teaspoons rice vinegar

2 teaspoons sesame oil

1 tablespoon hot water (125°F), plus more as needed

Baozi Wrappers (see page 206)

¼ cup avocado oil

1. Place the pork, ginger, and scallions in a mixing bowl and stir to combine. Place the remaining ingredients, except for the wrappers and avocado oil, in a separate bowl and stir until the salt and sugar have dissolved. Pour the liquid mixture over the pork mixture and stir to combine. Cover the mixing bowl and let the pork marinate for 30 minutes.

2. Place a wrapper in the palm of one hand and add about 1 tablespoon of the pork mixture. Cup the wrapper and close it over the filling. Squeeze it so that it is tightly sealed, and twist to remove any excess dough. Place the filled dumplings, seam side down, on a parchment-lined baking sheet and let them rise until doubled in size, about 30 minutes.

3. Place half of the avocado oil in a large cast-iron skillet and warm it over medium heat. Working in two batches to ensure that the dumplings are at least ½ inch apart, add the baozi to the pan, seam side up, and cook until golden brown, 1 to 2 minutes.

4. Add hot water to the skillet until it is ¼ inch deep, holding the cover of the pan in front of you to prevent being harmed by any oil splattering. Cover the pan and cook the dumplings until the water has evaporated, about 6 minutes. Remove the lid and cook until the bottoms of the dumplings are crispy, about 2 minutes. Remove the dumplings from the pan, transfer them to a plate, and cover loosely with aluminum foil. Repeat with the remaining dumplings and avocado oil.

5. Serve immediately with your favorite dipping sauce.

Okonomiyaki

This is sometimes referred to as "Japanese pizza," and while the comparison isn't particularly accurate, it does give some idea of how delicious and craveable okonomiyaki is.

3 tablespoons Worcestershire sauce

3½ tablespoons ketchup

2 tablespoons oyster sauce

1½ tablespoons plus ¼ teaspoon light brown sugar

1 cup all-purpose flour

½ teaspoon baking powder

½ teaspoon sea salt

½ cup peeled and grated mountain yam or potato

1 cup Dashi Stock (see page 207)

2 eggs, beaten

⅓ napa cabbage, shredded

1 tablespoon avocado oil, plus more as needed

½ cup minced shrimp

2 tablespoons Okonomiyaki Sauce (see page 208)

1 tablespoon Kewpie mayonnaise

Bonito flakes, for garnish

Toasted nori powder, for garnish

1. Place the Worcestershire sauce, ketchup, oyster sauce, and 1½ tablespoons of the brown sugar in a bowl and stir until well combined. Store the sauce in the refrigerator.

2. Place the flour, baking powder, salt, and remaining brown sugar in a mixing bowl and stir until well combined. Add the yam and dashi and stir until the mixture comes together as a batter. Chill the batter in the refrigerator for 1 hour.

3. Stir the eggs and cabbage into the chilled batter and set it aside.

4. Place the avocado oil in a large cast-iron skillet and warm it over medium-high heat. Ladle enough batter to make a 1-inch-thick pancake into the skillet, reduce the heat to medium, and cook until the bottom is set and golden brown, about 5 minutes.

5. Place the seafood on the uncooked side of the pancake and carefully transfer the pancake to a plate, with the uncooked side facing up. Add more avocado oil to the pan if it looks dry.

6. Invert the pan over the plate and flip the pancake over into the pan so that the uncooked side is now facing down. Cover the pan and cook until the pancake is cooked through and the edges are crispy, 3 to 4 minutes.

7. Transfer the cooked pancake to a plate and drizzle the sauce and mayonnaise over the top. Garnish the pancake with bonito flakes and toasted nori powder, slice it, and enjoy.

Dudhi Kofta

Serve these alongside a spicy, chile-spiked chutney or dipping sauce.

2 lbs. zucchini, trimmed and grated

2 teaspoons kosher salt

1 small red onion, chopped

¼ cup raw cashews

2 garlic cloves, minced

1-inch piece of fresh ginger, peeled and minced

4 bird's eye chili peppers, stems and seeds removed, minced

½ cup chickpea flour

2 tablespoons finely chopped fresh cilantro

Canola oil, as needed

1. Place the grated zucchini in a bowl, add the salt, and stir to combine. Let the mixture rest for 20 minutes.

2. Place the onion, cashews, garlic, ginger, and chilies in a food processor and blitz until the mixture is a chunky paste.

3. Place the zucchini in a linen towel and wring the towel to remove as much liquid from the zucchini as possible. Place the zucchini in a mixing bowl and add the onion-and-cashew paste. Stir to combine, add the chickpea flour and cilantro, and fold to incorporate. The dough should be slightly wet.

4. Add canola oil to a cast-iron Dutch oven until it is about 2 inches deep and warm it to 300°F over medium heat. As the oil warms, form tablespoons of the dough into balls and place them on a parchment-lined baking sheet. When the oil is ready, place the dumplings in the oil and fry until golden brown, about 5 minutes, turning the dumplings as necessary. Work in batches if necessary. Transfer the cooked dumplings to a paper towel–lined plate to drain.

ENTREES

Though it is more than capable of producing masterful sides, appetizers, and desserts, the entree is where cast-iron cookware truly shines, as it is where its versatility proves most valuable. Whether it be sliding a perfectly seared steak into the oven for a few moments to ensure that the interior is equally exceptional, quickly turning some seafood into a restaurant-quality meal, or allowing you to focus your energies elsewhere thanks to the long braises that are enabled by an enameled Dutch oven, cast iron always ensures that the main course will suit the shape of your day and still hit the mark in terms of execution.

Fried Catfish with Tennessee Tartar Sauce

Pro tip: whenever you add oil to a Dutch oven, fill it no more than halfway up the side of the pot, because when you add food to the oil, the level will rise.

4 lbs. catfish fillets, halved

Salt and pepper, to taste

2 cups buttermilk

1 tablespoon baking powder

¼ teaspoon cayenne pepper

2 cups cornmeal

3 tablespoons all-purpose flour

1 teaspoon garlic powder

Canola oil, as needed

Tennessee Tartar Sauce (see page 237), for serving

1. Season the catfish with salt and pepper, place it in a baking dish, and cover with the buttermilk. Chill in the refrigerator.

2. Place the baking powder, cayenne pepper, cornmeal, flour, garlic powder, a pinch of salt, and a pinch of pepper in a mixing bowl and whisk to combine. Set the mixture aside.

3. Add canola oil to a cast-iron Dutch oven until it fills the pot halfway. Bring to 350°F over medium-high heat. Place all of the ingredients in a mixing bowl, stir to combine, cover with plastic wrap, and store in the refrigerator until ready to serve.

4. Remove the catfish from the refrigerator, shake off any excess buttermilk, and dip each piece into the cornmeal mixture. Shake off any excess.

5. Working in batches, place the catfish in the oil and fry, while turning over halfway, until golden brown all over, about 8 minutes. Place the cooked pieces on a paper towel–lined plate. When all of the catfish has been cooked, serve with the tartar sauce.

Camarones en Adobo

A great recipe for a weeknight, as it is effortless to prepare, fresh-tasting, and vibrant.

---

4 guajillo chile peppers, stems and seeds removed

6 garlic cloves

2 small Roma tomatoes

3 tablespoons chipotles en adobo

Salt, to taste

1 lb. large shrimp, shells removed, deveined

¼ cup lard

Corn Tortillas (see page 214), for serving

White onion, chopped, for serving

Fresh cilantro, chopped, for serving

Lime wedges, for serving

1. Place the dried chiles in a dry, large cast-iron skillet and toast over medium heat until they darken and become fragrant and pliable. Submerge them in a bowl of hot water and let them soak for 15 to 20 minutes.

2. Drain the chiles and reserve the soaking liquid. Add the chiles to a blender along with the garlic, tomatoes, chipotles, and a small amount of the soaking liquid and puree until the mixture is a smooth paste. Season the adobo marinade with salt and let it cool completely.

3. Place the shrimp in the adobo and marinate for at least 20 to 30 minutes.

4. Place some of the lard in a large skillet and warm it over medium-high heat. Working in batches if needed to avoid crowding the pan, add the shrimp and cook until they are just firm and turn pink, 2 to 3 minutes. Add more lard to the pan if it starts to look dry.

5. Serve in tortillas with chopped onion, cilantro, and lime wedges.

Fried Trout Sandwiches

Edward Lee's take on the famous Vietnamese banh mi sandwich. Traditionally, banh mi is made with pork; this lighter version made with trout is fresh and crunchy.

FOR THE TEMPURA BATTER

1 cup all-purpose flour

1 tablespoon cornstarch

½ teaspoon kosher salt

1 large egg white

1 cup seltzer

FOR THE TROUT

Vegetable oil, as needed

4 (4 oz.) trout fillets

Salt and freshly ground black pepper, to taste

4 (6-inch) pieces of French baguette, for serving

Spicy Mayo (see page 242), for serving

1 head Bibb or Boston lettuce, leaves separated, for serving

Pear, Ginger & Cilantro Slaw (see page 243), for serving

1. To make the tempura batter: Combine the flour, cornstarch, and salt in a bowl. Whisk in the egg white and seltzer until a pancake-like batter forms. Do not over-whisk; small lumps are okay.

2. Heat ½ inch of oil to 375°F in a large cast-iron skillet over medium-high heat. Season both sides of the trout fillets with salt and pepper. Dip 2 fillets into the tempura batter to coat evenly, letting the excess drip off, and fry in the oil, turning once or twice, until golden and cooked through, 3 to 4 minutes. Drain on a paper towel–lined plate. The crust should be golden and flaky and the fish still moist inside. Keep the first batch warm and repeat with the remaining trout.

3. To assemble the sandwiches: Using a serrated knife, split the baguette pieces lengthwise in half. Spread some spicy mayo on both sides of each piece of bread. Layer the lettuce on the bottoms of the bread, then top with the trout and slaw. Gently cover with the other halves of baguette and serve.

Cochinita Pibil

This dish of slow-cooked pork is the signature dish of the Yucatán. It is somewhat similar to barbecue, but, in reality, is unlike any other dish in the world. Traditionally, it would be prepared in a stone-lined pit dug into the ground, but a cast-iron Dutch oven can ably fill in, making this delicious recipe accessible to all.

---

5 lbs. pork shoulder, cubed

Salt, to taste

Recado Rojo (see page 209)

1 package of banana leaves

1 large white onion, julienned

Lime wedges, for serving

Corn Tortillas (see page 214), warm, for serving

Fresh cilantro, chopped, for serving

Salsa de Chiltomate (see page 213), for serving

1. Place the pork shoulder in a large mixing bowl and season generously with salt. Pour the Recado Rojo over the pork and rub it all over. Place the pork in the refrigerator and let it marinate for 1 to 2 hours. If time allows, marinate for up to 24 hours.

2. Preheat the oven to 300°F. Remove the spines from the banana leaves and gently toast them over an open flame until pliable and bright green. Line a cast-iron Dutch oven with the banana leaves, place the pork on top, and cover the pork with the onion. Fold the banana leaves over the pork to create a packet. Cover the Dutch oven, place it in the oven, and roast until the pork is fork-tender, 2 to 3 hours.

3. Remove the lid from the Dutch oven and open up the banana leaf packet. Raise the oven's temperature to 400°F and roast for another 20 minutes. Serve with lime wedges, tortillas, cilantro, and Salsa de Chiltomate.

Darkly Braised Lamb Shoulder

Braising lamb coaxes out deep, hidden notes that yearn for dark flavors like chocolate and sorghum. Using a cast-iron Dutch oven makes all the difference in a recipe like this, allowing you to cook low and slow.

---

1. Make a rub mixing the salt and pepper together in a small bowl. Rub this all over the lamb shoulder and let sit at room temperature for about 30 minutes.

2. Heat the canola oil in a cast-iron Dutch oven over medium-high heat. Once the oil is hot, add the lamb shoulder and brown on all sides, about 3 minutes on each side.

3. Add all the vegetables to the pot, tucking them around the meat so they will brown a little. After about 3 minutes, add the bourbon, ketchup, soy sauce, balsamic vinegar, sorghum, black bean paste, chocolate, and stock. The liquid should completely cover the lamb; if it doesn't, add more stock or water to the pot. Bring this to a simmer over medium-high heat. Skim any foam that rises to the top. Lower the heat, put the lid on the pot, and simmer gently for 2½ hours.

4. Take the lid off the pot and cook for an additional 30 minutes. Check for the doneness: Does the lamb feel as if it will easily pull off the bone but is not so tender that it will turn to shreds when you try to lift it out of the pan? Good, it is done. Turn off the heat and let the lamb rest for about 15 minutes. (If you want, at this point you can cool and refrigerate this to reheat and serve at a later time; it will actually be better the next day.)

5. Transfer the lamb to a cutting board. Slice the meat against the grain or pull it off the bone in large chunks. Serve it over grits or rice in warm bowls. Ladle the braising liquid with the vegetables over the meat and serve immediately.

¼ cup kosher salt

2 tablespoons freshly ground black pepper

1 lamb shoulder roast (3 pounds)

2 tablespoons canola oil

1 cup chopped onions

1 cup chopped carrots

1 cup chopped celery

3 garlic cloves, minced

1 cup chopped button mushrooms

1 jalapeño pepper, chopped (seeds and all)

½ cup bourbon

¼ cup ketchup

1 tablespoon soy sauce

1 tablespoon balsamic vinegar

3 tablespoons sorghum

¼ cup black bean paste

1½ ounces bittersweet chocolate, chopped

6 cups Chicken Stock (see page 212), or as needed

Cooked grits or rice, for serving

Ramp & Fiddlehead Fried Rice

Fiddleheads are the very beginning of ferns that are still coiled, the most coveted of which come from the ostrich fern. When cooked properly, they still have a little crunch—like perfectly cooked asparagus (which make a fine substitute in a pinch)—and taste the way fresh ferns smell: grassy and earthy and herbaceous.

2 cups rice (ideally black, but brown will work too)

Salt and pepper, to taste

¼ cup extra-virgin olive oil, plus more for drizzling

6 ramps, sliced

¾ lb. fiddleheads, cut into 1½-inch pieces and blanched

3 tablespoons seasoned rice wine vinegar, plus more for drizzling

4 large eggs, fried

Microgreens, for garnish

1. First, cook the rice according to the manufacturer's directions. Rinse the cooked rice with cold water, drain well, and spread over a baking sheet. Chill in the refrigerator for a few hours or overnight (this will help it get nice and crispy when you fry it).

2. Heat 2 tablespoons of olive oil in a large cast-iron skillet over medium-high heat. Add the ramps and fiddleheads, ½ teaspoon salt, and a few twists of fresh pepper. Sauté until the greens have wilted and the whites have just begun to brown, about 2 minutes.

3. Raise the heat to high and add the remaining 2 tablespoons olive oil and the rice. Let it be without stirring for 15 to 20 seconds, then give the pan a good stir or shake. Continue frying the rice, stirring occasionally, until crisp, about 4 minutes. Add the vinegar, give the pan another good stir, and remove from the heat.

4. Toss the microgreens, with a drizzle of olive oil, a splash of vinegar, and a pinch of salt.

5. Divide the fried rice among 4 plates, top each plate with a fried egg, and garnish with the microgreens and a twist of black pepper.

Pasta Amatriciana

Amatriciana is, without a doubt, the queen of Roman pastas—carbonara is a relatively new addition to osteria menus, while amatriciana has been there for centuries.

---

6 ripe San Marzano tomatoes

1 tablespoon extra-virgin olive oil

4½ oz. guanciale (guanciale amatriciano preferred), cut into 1-inch-long and ¼-inch-wide strips

1 piece of chile pepper

2 tablespoons dry white wine

Salt, to taste

1 lb. spaghetti

1 (heaping) cup grated pecorino cheese, plus more for serving

1. Bring water to a boil in a large saucepan. Add the tomatoes and boil them for 2 minutes. Drain the tomatoes and let them cool. When they are cool enough to handle, peel the tomatoes, remove the seeds, and chop the remaining flesh. Set the tomatoes aside.

2. Place the olive oil in a large cast-iron skillet and warm it over medium heat. Add the guanciale and chile and cook until the guanciale starts to render its fat. Raise the heat to medium-high and cook until the guanciale has browned.

3. Add the wine and cook until it has evaporated.

4. Remove the guanciale from the pan with a slotted spoon. Set it aside.

5. Add the tomatoes to the pan, season with salt, and reduce the heat to medium. Cook for 2 minutes.

6. Remove the chile, return the guanciale to the pan, and gently simmer the sauce.

7. Bring water to a boil in a large saucepan. Add salt, let the water return to a full boil, and add the pasta. Cook the pasta until it is al dente. Drain the pasta and place it in a bowl.

8. Add the pecorino to the bowl and toss to combine. Add the sauce, toss to combine, and serve with additional pecorino.

Cornmeal-Dusted Grouper with Herb Puree

As the cornmeal toasts and browns in the hot skillet, it gives off an aroma reminiscent of cornbread, which is never a bad thing. This herb puree is amazing with fish, but you can add it to almost any dish for a burst of bright, fresh flavor.

FOR THE PUREE

Kosher salt, to taste

1 cup tightly packed mixed herb leaves (such as basil and parsley)

¼ teaspoon grated garlic

2 tablespoons extra-virgin olive oil

FOR THE GROUPER

1 cup fine white cornmeal

2 tablespoons kosher salt, plus more to taste

2 teaspoons freshly ground white pepper, plus more to taste

4 (6 oz.) skinless grouper fillets (each about ¾ inch thick)

2 tablespoons canola oil

Fresh herbs, for garnish (optional)

Edible flowers, for garnish (optional)

1. For the herb puree: Bring a large saucepan of salted water to a boil over high heat. Make an ice bath with equal parts ice and water in a large bowl. Put the herb leaves in a large mesh strainer and submerge them in the boiling water until tender and bright green, about 30 seconds. Leaving them in the strainer, transfer the herbs to the ice bath and submerge until completely cold. Remove from the ice bath, shake off the excess water, and drain the leaves on paper towels. Reserve ¼ cup of the ice water.

2. Combine the herbs, garlic, and reserved ¼ cup water in a blender and blend on high until completely smooth, about 1 minute. With the blender running on low, slowly drizzle in the olive oil. Blend in ½ teaspoon salt. Transfer to a container, cover, and set aside. (The herb puree can be made ahead. Tightly covered, it will keep for up to 1 day in the refrigerator. Remove from the refrigerator 30 minutes before using.)

3. For the grouper: Combine the cornmeal, salt, and white pepper in a large shallow bowl and mix well. Season the grouper fillets liberally with salt and white pepper. Dredge the fillets in the cornmeal, gently shaking off any excess, and put them on a large plate.

4. Line a rimmed baking sheet with paper towels. Heat the canola oil in a large cast-iron skillet over medium-high heat until it shimmers. Place the fillets in the skillet skinned side up and sear them for 2 minutes, without moving them. Reduce the heat to medium and cook until the fillets are golden brown on the first side, about 3 minutes. (Peek under the fillet to check.) Turn them over and continue to cook just until the flesh flakes when gently prodded with a fork, 3 to 4 minutes. Transfer the fillets to the prepared baking sheet to drain briefly.

5. To serve: Place a grouper fillet on each of the four warm plates. Spoon the herb puree next to the fillets. Garnish with the herbs and flowers, if using.

YIELD: 4 Servings / **ACTIVE TIME:** 15 Minutes / **TOTAL TIME:** 35 Minutes

Espresso-Rubbed Pork Tenderloin with Sour Cherry Glaze

Pork tenderloin is a blank canvas—you have to bring the flavor to it, but it plays well with a surprising number of elements.

3 lbs. pork tenderloin, trimmed

2 tablespoons extra-virgin olive oil, plus more as needed

1 tablespoon instant espresso powder

1 tablespoon ancho chile powder

1 tablespoon paprika

1 tablespoon brown sugar

1 teaspoon kosher salt

Black pepper, to taste

Sour Cherry Glaze (see page 238)

1. Preheat the oven to 400°F. Remove the silver skin and any excess fat from the tenderloins. Rub the pork with the olive oil.

2. Combine the espresso powder, ancho chile powder, paprika, brown sugar, salt, and pepper in a small bowl. Rub the pork tenderloins with the mixture, covering as much of the surface as possible.

3. Warm a large cast-iron skillet over medium heat. Add enough olive oil to coat the bottom. When the oil starts to shimmer, add the tenderloins and sear on all sides, about 5 minutes total.

4. Place the skillet in the oven and roast until the internal temperature of the tenderloins is 145°F, about 15 minutes. Remove from the oven, place the tenderloins on a cutting board, loosely tent with foil, and let them sit for 10 to 15 minutes.

5. Drizzle the Sour Cherry Glaze on top and serve.

YIELD: 2 Servings / **ACTIVE TIME:** 15 Minutes / **TOTAL TIME:** 30 Minutes

Herb-Crusted Cod with Caper Cream

Make this dish when something quick and easy is all the day will allow for, as the preparation doesn't require much work, and the outcome is assured to be delicious.

---

1 lb. cod loin, cut into 4 pieces

1½ cups panko

1 tablespoon chopped fresh parsley, plus more for garnish

1 tablespoon chopped fresh chives, plus more for garnish

1 tablespoon chopped fresh basil, plus more for garnish

Salt and pepper, to taste

2 tablespoons canola oil

Caper Cream (see page 228)

Lemon wedges, for serving

1. Preheat the oven to 400°F. Pat the cod dry with paper towels. Place the panko and fresh herbs in a food processor, season with salt and pepper, and pulse to combine. Set the mixture aside.

2. Place the canola oil in a large cast-iron skillet and warm it over high heat. Season the cod with salt and pepper and dredge one side in the panko mixture. Place it in the pan, panko topping facing up, reduce the heat to medium, and cook until the edges of the cod start to brown.

3. Transfer the cod to the oven and roast until it is cooked through and the topping is golden brown, 6 to 8 minutes.

4. Remove the pan from the oven. Using a fish spatula, carefully remove the fish from the pan and place it in a serving dish.

5. Spoon the Caper Cream into the dish, garnish with fresh herbs, and serve with lemon wedges.

Herb-Crusted Cod with Caper Cream
see page 101

Chicken Breasts with Peanut Butter Gravy

Sean Brock: "The taste of crispy-skinned pan-roasted chicken with pan gravy will never, ever get old to me. The big lesson from this recipe is to salt the chicken ahead of time. Letting the breasts air-dry in the refrigerator wicks away the excess moisture that can keep the skin from crisping up in the pan."

1. For the chicken: Liberally season the chicken breasts with salt, place on a rack set over a nonreactive baking dish, and refrigerate, uncovered, for 24 hours.

2. The next day, remove the chicken from the refrigerator and leave at room temperature for 30 minutes before cooking. Preheat the oven to 350°F.

3. Heat the canola oil in a large cast-iron skillet over medium-high heat until it shimmers. Pat the chicken breasts dry with paper towels and season them liberally with pepper. Place the chicken breasts in the skillet skin side down and sear until the skin is golden and crispy, about 4 minutes.

4. Add the thyme sprigs to the skillet, turn the breast over, transfer the skillet to the oven, and roast for about 10 minutes, until an instant-read thermometer inserted in the thickest part of a breast reads 140°F. Transfer the chicken to the cutting board, lightly cover with aluminum foil, and rest for 5 minutes. Remove the thyme from the skillet and set the skillet aside.

5. For the gravy: There should be about 1½ tablespoons of fat left in the skillet from cooking the chicken; add a little more oil if you need to. Place the skillet over medium heat, add the onion, and cook, stirring occasionally, until it starts to soften. Stir in the flour and cook, stirring constantly, until the flour just begins to turn a light golden color, about 2 minutes. Slowly stir in the milk and chicken stock and bring to a simmer, stirring constantly. Reduce the heat to low, stir in the peanut butter, peanut oil, lime juice, and pepper, and return the gravy to a simmer. Season lightly with salt, remove from the stove, and set aside.

6. To complete: Combine the parsley, mint, peanuts, 2 teaspoons of green peanut oil, and the lime juice in a small bowl. Season lightly with salt and pepper and toss to combine. Keeping the skin on, carefully carve the chicken away from the bones; discard the bones. Slice each breast crosswise into ¾-inch-thick slices. Using a pastry brush, lightly brush the slices with the remaining 2 teaspoons green peanut oil and sprinkle with a few grains of finishing salt.

7. Spoon some of the gravy into the center of each of four warm plates and place a sliced chicken breast on each. Divide the herb salad among the plates and serve.

FOR THE CHICKEN

4 (10 oz.) skin-on, bone-in chicken breasts

Kosher salt, to taste

1 tablespoon canola oil, or as needed

Freshly ground black pepper, to taste

5 sprigs of fresh thyme

FOR THE GRAVY

¼ cup very finely diced sweet onion

1½ tablespoons all-purpose flour

½ cup whole milk

½ cup Chicken Stock (see page 212)

¼ cup plus 2 tablespoons creamy peanut butter

1 tablespoon plus 2 teaspoons Oliver Farm Green Peanut Oil

1 teaspoon fresh lime juice

¾ teaspoon freshly ground black pepper

Kosher salt, to taste

¾ cup fresh flat-leaf parsley leaves

½ cup fresh mint leaves

¼ cup shelled green peanuts (about 4 ounces in the shell), roughly chopped

4 teaspoons Oliver Farm Green Peanut Oil

1 teaspoon fresh lime juice

Kosher salt and freshly ground black pepper, to taste

Coarse finishing salt, for garnish

Squid Stuffed with Sausage

Stuffing squid is a no-brainer. Their bodies even look like sausage casings. You just put in your stuffing, brown the squid in a cast-iron skillet, and finish them off in the oven.

¼ cup extra-virgin olive oil

1 tablespoon seasoned rice wine vinegar

1 teaspoon Dijon mustard

1 tablespoon finely chopped shallot

Salt and pepper, to taste

1 lb. cleaned fresh squid (about a dozen bodies and tentacles), rinsed under cold water

1 lb. sausage, casing removed

3 tablespoons unsalted butter

½ lb. young mustard greens

Mustard (preferably Chinese spicy mustard), for serving

1. Preheat the oven to 425°F.

2. Make the vinaigrette by whisking together 3 tablespoons of olive oil, the vinegar, mustard, and shallot. Season to taste with salt and pepper and set aside.

3. Gently stuff each squid body with about a tablespoon of sausage.

4. Heat the remaining tablespoon of olive oil in a large cast-iron skillet over medium-high heat. When the oil starts to smoke, add the squid bodies and cook, turning once, until just golden brown, about 2 minutes per side.

5. Add the tentacles to the skillet along with the butter. Transfer the pan to the oven and roast until the sausage is cooked through, 6 to 8 minutes.

6. Toss the greens with vinaigrette and serve with the hot squid, along with mustard.

YIELD: 2 Servings / **ACTIVE TIME:** 10 Minutes / **TOTAL TIME:** 20 Minutes

Crispy Salmon with Red Chermoula

Chermoula, a North African condiment, is great with seafood, and exceptional with salmon prepared in this manner.

---

1 tablespoon canola oil

1 lb. skin-on salmon fillets, cut into 4 oz. pieces

Salt and pepper, to taste

2 tablespoons unsalted butter

3 sprigs of fresh thyme

2 garlic cloves, crushed

½ lemon

Red Chermoula Sauce (see page 230)

Fresh herbs, finely chopped, for garnish

1. Preheat the oven to 450°F. Place the canola oil in a large cast-iron skillet and warm it over medium-high heat. Season the salmon with salt and pepper and carefully place it in the pan, skin side down. Place the pan in the oven and roast it for 3 to 4 minutes, depending on the thickness of the pieces of salmon.

2. Remove the pan from the oven and add the butter, thyme, and garlic. Baste the salmon with the butter until its internal temperature is 135°F.

3. Squeeze the juice of the lemon into the pan and baste the salmon a few more times.

4. Transfer the salmon to a paper towel–lined plate to drain briefly.

5. Place the salmon on the serving plates, drizzle the chermoula over the top, garnish with fresh herbs, and serve.

YIELD: 10 Servings / ACTIVE TIME: 40 Minutes / TOTAL TIME: 3 Hours

Cappone Ripieno

Common in Central and Northern Italy but most popular in Piedmont, cappone ripieno is a stuffed capon, a castrated cock that is known to be particularly tasty due to its fatty, tender flesh.

¼ cup extra-virgin olive oil, plus more as needed

4½ lb. whole capon

7 oz. ground veal

7 oz. ground Italian sausage

1½ cups fresh bread crumbs

1 cup grated Parmesan cheese

2 eggs

1 white onion, finely diced

1 garlic clove, minced

Handful of fresh parsley, finely chopped

Handful of fresh sage, finely chopped

1 teaspoon finely chopped fresh rosemary

Freshly grated nutmeg, to taste

Salt and pepper, to taste

1 cup dry white wine

1 cup Beef Stock (see page 211)

1. Preheat the oven to 355°F and coat a large cast-iron skillet with olive oil. Remove the capon's innards and rinse out the cavity.

2. Place the veal, sausage, bread crumbs, Parmesan, eggs, onion, garlic, parsley, sage, rosemary, and olive oil in a large bowl, season with nutmeg, salt, and pepper, and work the mixture with your hands until well combined.

3. Stuff the capon with the mixture and tie it closed with kitchen twine. Season the capon with salt, place it in the pan, and place it in the oven.

4. Combine the wine and stock in a bowl. Roast the capon until it is cooked through, about 2 hours, basting it with the wine mixture frequently and turning it occasionally, making sure not to pierce the flesh when you do.

5. Remove the capon from the oven, slice, and serve.

YIELD: 2 Servings / **ACTIVE TIME:** 20 Minutes / **TOTAL TIME:** 30 Minutes

Roasted Duck Breast with Cranberry Mostarda & Crispy Kale

Remember that the key to successfully cooking duck breasts is to score the skin, as it helps the fat render and allows the skin to become crispy.

---

4 oz. fresh cranberries

2 red apples, cored and chopped

¼ cup sugar

2 teaspoons diced shallot

1 teaspoon apple cider vinegar

2 teaspoons kosher salt, plus more to taste

1 lb. skin-on duck breasts

Black pepper, to taste

1 tablespoon unsalted butter

Cranberry Mostarda (see page 220), for serving

Crispy Kale (see page 221), for serving

1. Place the cranberries, apples, sugar, shallot, vinegar, and salt in a small saucepan and cook over medium heat until the cranberries are soft and the mixture has reduced slightly.

2. Strain the mixture, reserving the liquid, and place it in a blender. Puree until smooth, adding the reserved liquid as needed to get the desired consistency. Set the puree aside.

3. Trim any excess fat from the duck and score the skin with a sharp knife. Season the skin side with salt, turn the duck over, and season the flesh side with salt and pepper.

4. Place the duck, skin side down, in a large cast-iron skillet and cook it over medium-low heat until the fat starts to render. Drain all of the fat that collects in the pan and closely monitor the heat so that the skin doesn't get too brown before it has a chance to become crispy.

5. When the duck's skin is crispy, turn it over and cook for 2 minutes. Add the butter and baste the duck until the internal temperature is about 130ºF.

6. Remove the duck from the pan and let it rest for a few minutes.

7. Spread some puree over each of the serving plates. Slice the duck, set it atop the puree, and serve with the Cranberry Mostarda and Crispy Kale.

**Roasted Duck Breast with
Cranberry Mostarda & Crispy Kale**
see page 111

T-Bone Steak with Lemongrass-Habanero Marinade

Edward Lee: "One problem I find with a big steak is that after a few bites, it starts to taste dull. So I like to add a bright acidic marinade for a contrast with all the meatiness. The acid actually accentuates the umami element in the steak and gives it a punch that is quite addictive."

6 garlic cloves

3 lemongrass stalks, trimmed to within 2 inches of the root end and finely minced

2 habanero peppers, halved and seeds removed

Juice of 1 lemon

Juice of 1 orange

2 tablespoons sesame oil

1 teaspoon soy sauce

½ teaspoon salt, plus more to taste

Black pepper, to taste

2 (10 oz.) T-bone steaks (each ¾ inch thick)

1 tablespoon unsalted butter

1 teaspoon peanut oil

1. Place all of the ingredients, except for the steaks, butter, and peanut oil, in a blender and blend on high until well blended.

2. Generously salt and pepper the steaks. Place in a glass baking dish and pour the marinade over the steaks. Marinate at room temperature for 20 minutes.

3. In a large cast-iron skillet, heat the butter and peanut oil over high heat until just barely smoking. Add the steaks, cover the pan with a lid, and cook for 3 minutes. Uncover, flip the steaks, and reduce the heat to medium. Cook the steaks, uncovered, for another 2 minutes or so. Do the steaks look caramelized and moist and shiny from the marinade? Good, they are ready to eat. Remove the steaks from the pan and let them rest on a cutting board for 2 minutes.

4. Spoon the pan juices over the steaks; serve immediately.

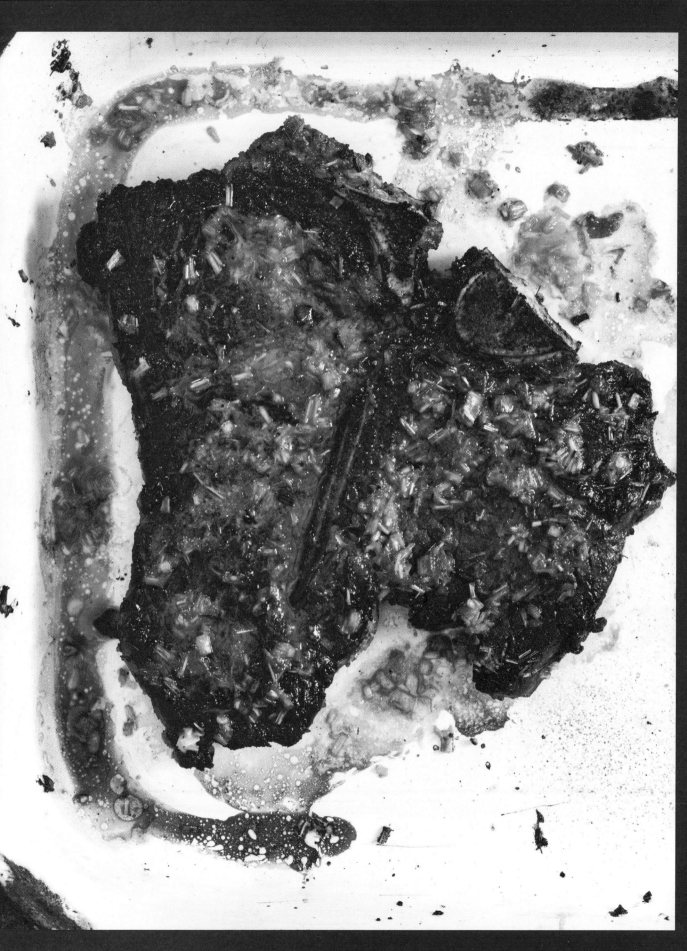

YIELD: 6 to 8 Servings / **ACTIVE TIME:** 40 Minutes / **TOTAL TIME:** 6 Hours

Pork with Blue Cheese Polenta

The peach-spiked hot sauce takes this comforting dish to an entirely different level.

---

1. Preheat the oven to 300°F. Season the pork shoulder generously with salt and pepper. Place the pork shoulder in a large cast-iron skillet and cook over medium-high heat until it is browned all over, turning it as necessary. Transfer the pork shoulder to a cast-iron Dutch oven and add the onion, bay leaves, paprika, brown sugar, peppercorns, 4 cups of the stock, and mustard.

2. Cover the Dutch oven and place in the oven until the pork is fork-tender, about 4 hours.

3. Remove the pork from the oven, let it cool slightly, and then shred with a fork.

4. Approximately 1 hour before the pulled pork will be finished cooking, place the cornmeal, the remaining 3 cups of stock, and the water in a large pot. Bring to a boil over medium-high heat, reduce heat so that the mixture simmers, and cook, while stirring frequently, until the mixture is thick, about 40 minutes to 1 hour.

5. Add half of the butter and stir to combine. Stir half of the blue cheese into the pot, season with salt and pepper, and remove from heat. Set aside.

6. Once you have removed the pork shoulder from the oven, raise the oven temperature to 400°F.

7. Arrange the peaches skin side down on a baking sheet and place them in the oven. Cook until they begin to darken, about 10 minutes. You can also grill the peaches if you're after a slightly smokier sauce. Remove the peaches from the oven and place them in a medium saucepan. Add the vinegar, sugar, garlic, peppers, and lemon juice and bring to a simmer over medium-low heat. Simmer for 10 minutes, transfer the mixture to a blender, and puree until smooth.

8. Stir the remaining butter into the polenta and spoon the polenta into warmed bowls. Lay some of the pulled pork over it, top with the hot sauce and remaining blue cheese, and serve.

6- to 8-lb., bone-in pork shoulder

Salt and pepper, to taste

1 large onion, diced

3 bay leaves

2 teaspoons paprika

¼ cup brown sugar

2 tablespoons whole peppercorns

7 cups Chicken Stock (see page 212)

1 tablespoon mustard

2 cups cornmeal

2 cups water

½ cup unsalted butter

1 cup crumbled blue cheese

8 overripe peaches, pitted and quartered

2 cups apple cider vinegar

¾ cup sugar

3 garlic cloves, chopped

6 jalapeño chile peppers, stems and seeds removed, diced

4 cayenne peppers, stems and seeds removed, diced

1 large Yukon Gold potato
(about 11 ounces), peeled

1 tablespoon unsalted butter

2½ teaspoons kosher salt

¾ teaspoon freshly ground black
pepper

3 to 3½ lb. whole chicken

2 teaspoons extra-virgin olive oil

Potato-Stuffed Roast Chicken

Edward Lee: "The perfect roasted chicken had always eluded me. There's no way to cook the thighs through without drying out the breast. I had gone through all the recipes I could try, but I'd never quite felt satisfied with any of them. Then I started trying out the technique in this recipe in the privacy of my home kitchen. It makes sense: the potatoes insulate the breasts, the fat from the skin flavors the potatoes, and the breasts stay incredibly moist."

1. Using the large holes of a box grater, grate the potato onto the cutting board. Wrap the grated potato in a square of cheesecloth and wring out as much water as possible.

2. Melt the butter in a large cast-iron skillet over medium heat. Add the grated potatoes, season with ½ teaspoon of salt and ¼ teaspoon of pepper, stir gently with a wooden spoon, and cook for exactly 2 minutes, not longer. Quickly transfer the potatoes to a plate and let cool.

3. Position a rack in the upper third of the oven and preheat the oven to 400°F.

4. Place the chicken on your work surface with the legs facing you. Starting at the tail end of each breast, use your fingers to gently loosen the skin from the flesh. Slide one finger in between the breast meat and the skin and move it from side to side to release the skin from the meat. Yes, this will feel funny, but carry on. Be careful not to tear the skin, but if it does rip a little, don't worry; it's not the end of the world. Rotate the bird so the breast is now facing you and do the same thing starting at the neck end of the breast, so that all of the breast skin is released from the meat.

5. Gently stuff the cooled potatoes into the space between the skin and breasts: Stuff half of them from the top and the remaining potatoes from the bottom. Now even out the potato layer: Place both your hands over the skin of the breasts and massage it to smooth and flatten the potatoes into an even layer. Rub the chicken with olive oil and season with the remaining 2 teaspoons salt and ½ teaspoon pepper.

6. Wipe out the cast-iron skillet with a paper towel and heat it over medium heat. Place the chicken breast side down in the hot skillet, press it gently against the bottom of the pan, and hold it there for a bit while it browns lightly, about 3 minutes. Gently flip the chicken onto its back; the skin on top should be lightly browned. Slide the skillet into the oven and cook for 50 minutes to 1 hour. To check for doneness, insert an instant-read thermometer into the upper part of a thigh. I like my chicken when the thigh meat is at 155°F, but you may want yours at 160°F if you don't like any pink at all. Allow the chicken to rest in the pan for 10 minutes.

7. Transfer the chicken to a cutting board. Cut each breast away from the bones, being careful not to disturb the potatoes under the crispy skin. Slice each breast into 3 chunks and arrange on a platter. Carve the legs and add them to the platter, along with the wings.

Skillet Mussels with Rosemary, Lavender & Lime

Erin French: "This dish is about to become an all-time favorite entertaining staple of yours. It's got just five ingredients and one pan, and yet it's pure flavor—not to mention a very sexy plate of food."

---

2 lbs. mussels, rinsed well

4 sprigs of fresh rosemary

1 small handful of fresh lavender

½ cup unsalted butter

2 limes, halved

1. Over a hot fire, or high heat on your stove, heat a large cast-iron skillet. Dump in the mussels in a single layer and top with the rosemary and lavender. Let the pan sit undisturbed, and uncovered, until the mussels begin to open their shells, 1½ to 2 minutes.

2. Dot the butter around the skillet and begin to shake it back and forth over the heat. It will sizzle and smoke as the butter melts. Continue to shake the skillet until the mussels are fully open, 1 to 2 minutes.

3. Remove the pan from the heat, squeeze the lime halves over the mussels, and serve immediately, in the skillet, with a serving spoon.

Chilorio

A spicy and flavorful dish of tender pulled pork. This is perfect for serving family style with warm tortillas or arroz a la Mexicana.

---

4 lbs. boneless pork shoulder, cut into 4 pieces

Salt, to taste

2 tablespoons extra-virgin olive oil

4 guajillo chile peppers, stems and seeds removed

2 ancho chile peppers, stems and seeds removed

6 garlic cloves

¼ white onion

2 cups orange juice

¼ cup white vinegar

1 tablespoon dried Mexican oregano

1½ teaspoons cumin

1½ teaspoons black pepper

Corn Tortillas (see page 214), warm, for serving (optional)

Arroz a la Mexicana, for serving (optional)

1. Season the pork with salt and let it sit at room temperature while you prepare the sauce.

2. Place the olive oil in a cast-iron Dutch oven and warm it over medium heat. Add the chiles and fry until fragrant.

3. Transfer the chiles to a blender, add the remaining ingredients, except for the tortillas or rice, and puree until smooth.

4. Working with one piece of pork at a time, place it in the Dutch oven and sear until browned on all sides.

5. Pour the puree over the pork. If the pork is not covered, add water until it is.

6. Cover the Dutch oven and cook the pork over low heat until tender and falling apart, about 2 hours.

7. Serve with the sauce and warm tortillas or rice.

Chilorio
see page 121

Il Cif e Ciaf

This is a traditional pork-based dish from Abruzzi that uses those parts of the pig that are not suitable to become cured pork.

½ cup extra-virgin olive oil

1 sprig of fresh rosemary

3 bay leaves

2½ lbs. assorted cuts of pork (bacon, ribs, lean cuts, etc.)

1 cup dry white wine

Salt and pepper, to taste

10 garlic cloves, peeled

2 dried chile peppers, stems and seeds removed, torn

Crusty bread, toasted, for serving

1. Place the olive oil in a large cast-iron skillet and warm it over medium-high heat. Add the rosemary and bay leaves and cook for 1 minute.

2. Add the pork to the pan and sear until it is browned all over, turning it as necessary.

3. Deglaze the pan with the wine, scraping up any browned bits from the bottom. Cook until the wine has evaporated, cover the pan, and reduce the heat to low. Cook, stirring occasionally, for 30 minutes.

4. Remove the bay leaves and discard them. Season the dish with salt and pepper and check to see if the pork is sticking to the pan. If it is, add 1 cup water, cover the pan, and cook for another 30 minutes.

5. Preheat the oven to 390°F.

6. Add the garlic and peppers, transfer the pan to the oven, and braise the pork until it is very tender, about 20 minutes.

7. Remove the pan from the oven and serve with toasted bread.

YIELD: *4 Servings* / ACTIVE TIME: *45 Minutes* / TOTAL TIME: *2 Hours*

Braised Turkey Leg, Hot Brown–Style

Edward Lee: "Because the dish is so devilishly filling, it needs a spicy bourbon with a few cubes of ice in a large rocks glass."

---

4 slices of thick-cut bacon, finely diced, plus more, extra crispy, for garnish

2 tablespoons unsalted butter

2 bone-in turkey drumsticks (about 2 lbs.)

Sea salt and freshly ground black pepper, to taste

2 carrots, peeled and finely diced

2 celery stalks, finely diced

2 leeks, white part only, finely chopped

3 tablespoons sorghum

2 cups apple cider

1 cup Chicken Stock (see page 212)

2 sprigs of fresh sage

2 slices of Texas toast (regular white bread works fine too), cut into rectangular ½-inch-thick croutons

⅔ cup grated semi-firm cheese (such as Gouda)

½ cup diced tomato, for garnish

Fresh sage, chopped, for garnish

Fresh thyme, chopped, for garnish

Smoked paprika, for garnish

1. Preheat the oven to 325°F.

2. Warm a large cast-iron skillet over medium heat. Add the bacon and cook until it renders its fat and begins to crisp, 4 to 6 minutes. Remove the bacon and drain on a paper towel; leave the bacon fat in the pan.

3. Add the butter to the pan and melt over medium heat. Season the turkey legs generously with salt and pepper. Add to the pan and brown on all sides, 8 to 10 minutes. Transfer the turkey legs to a plate.

4. Pour off all but 2 tablespoons of the fat from the pan. Add the carrots, celery, and leeks and cook, stirring occasionally, until they begin to brown, about 5 minutes.

5. Add the bacon and turkey legs to the pan, then add the sorghum, apple cider, and chicken stock and bring to a simmer. Add the sage, cover with the lid, and transfer to the oven. Bake for 45 minutes.

6. Check the turkey legs. If they're not totally immersed in liquid, flip them over and replace the lid. Cook for an additional 35 minutes, or until the meat is falling off the bone. Transfer the turkey to a plate and let cool slightly. Set the braising liquid aside. (Leave the oven on.)

7. Meanwhile, spread the croutons on a baking sheet and toast in the oven for 8 to 10 minutes, just until slightly browned. Remove from the oven.

8. Pull the skin off the turkey legs and discard. Remove the meat from the bones and shred it with your hands.

9. To serve, divide the braised turkey meat among four bowls. Add the cheese to the braising liquid and whisk until combined, then season with salt and pepper. Ladle about ½ cup of the braising liquid into each bowl. Top each serving with some croutons, a spoonful of the diced tomato, a pinch of the fresh herbs, and some additional bacon. Dust each bowl with paprika and serve immediately.

Adobo-Fried Chicken & Waffles

This is a Filipino adobo, not the Spanish version. The vinegar brightens the richness of the fried chicken and helps with digestion. Add more or fewer chiles, depending on how much heat you like.

1. To make the waffles: Preheat your waffle maker and lightly oil it. Meanwhile, in a medium bowl, whisk together the flour, sugar, baking powder, salt, paprika, and black pepper. In a small bowl, whisk together the melted butter, eggs, and buttermilk. Pour the wet ingredients into the dry ingredients a little at a time, whisking constantly.

2. Cook the waffles according to your waffle maker's instructions. Cut the waffles into 2-inch-wide wedges and reserve on a plate at room temperature or keep warm in a low oven until ready to serve.

3. To make the chicken: Place the adobo in a large pot, cover with a tight-fitting lid, and bring to a simmer over medium heat. Simmer for 5 minutes, then turn the heat down as low as it will go.

4. Arrange the chicken pieces on a work surface and season them with salt. Add the chicken pieces to gently simmering broth, cover, and poach for 15 minutes, turning once halfway through. You want the chicken to poach gently and stay moist while picking up the flavor of the broth, so make sure the liquid does not get hotter than a gentle simmer. Turn off the heat and allow the chicken to cool in the liquid, covered, for about 20 minutes.

5. Remove the chicken pieces from the adobo broth (discard the broth) and transfer the chicken to a plate lined with paper towels. Pat dry.

6. To fry the chicken: Pour the buttermilk into a large shallow bowl. In another bowl, combine the flour, 1 teaspoon salt, the paprika, and the pepper. Dip each chicken piece in the buttermilk, shake off any excess liquid, dredge in the flour mixture, turning to coat, and transfer to a large plate. Let stand at room temperature for 15 minutes. The flour coating will turn a little soft— that's a good thing.

7. Meanwhile, fill a large, deep cast-iron skillet about halfway with peanut oil. Heat the oil to 365°F. Cook the chicken pieces 2 or 3 at a time for 8 to 10 minutes, turning every minute or so, depending on how thick the pieces of chicken are; wings will cook faster and drumsticks will take the longest. Be sure to keep the oil temperature at around 350°F to 365°F. The chicken is cooked when the internal temperature reaches at least 165°F. Using tongs, lift the chicken out of the oil and drain on paper towels. Season again with a little salt, and transfer to a platter.

8. Serve the fried chicken with the waffles and the dipping sauce. Eat it hot!

FOR THE WAFFLES

2 cups all-purpose flour

1 teaspoon sugar

1 teaspoon baking powder

½ teaspoon kosher salt

¼ teaspoon paprika

¼ teaspoon freshly ground black pepper

3 tablespoons unsalted butter, melted and cooled

2 large eggs

1 cup buttermilk

FOR THE CHICKEN

Adobo Broth (see page 240)

2 lbs. chicken, thighs and/or drumsticks, plus wings if desired (do not use breasts)

Salt

2 cups buttermilk

1 cup all-purpose flour

1 teaspoon paprika

½ teaspoon freshly ground black pepper

Peanut oil, as needed

Chicken & Waffle Dipping Sauce (see page 239)

YIELD: 4 Servings / ACTIVE TIME: 20 Minutes / TOTAL TIME: 40 Minutes

Creole Smash Burgers

A burger is wonderful in its classic form, but it is also very accommodating, allowing the imaginative cook to incorporate their favorite flavors and ingredients. These burgers are a perfect example, freighted with the flavors that make Haitian food so special.

---

1 lb. ground beef

1 tablespoon Epis (see page 217)

2 tablespoons diced bell pepper

2 tablespoons diced onion

1 teaspoon adobo seasoning

2 teaspoons garlic powder

1 teaspoon black pepper, plus more to taste

Salt, to taste

3 tablespoons canola oil

4 slices of cheddar cheese

2 tablespoons unsalted butter

4 Seeded Buttermilk Buns (see page 215), split open

Spicy Mayo (see page 242)

8 slices of bacon, cooked

1. Place the ground beef, Epis, bell pepper, onion, adobo seasoning, garlic powder, and black pepper in a mixing bowl, season with salt, and stir until well combined.

2. Divide the mixture into 4½ oz. portions, form them into balls, and set them aside.

3. Place the canola oil in a large cast-iron skillet and warm it over medium-high heat. Season the tops of the burgers with salt and pepper and place them in the pan, seasoned side down. If your pan is not large enough to comfortably fit all of the burgers at once, cook them in batches, as you want to provide them plenty of room in the pan.

4. Using a small cast-iron skillet or a burger press, smash the burgers flat. Season the tops of the burgers with salt and pepper as they cook. Sear the burgers until they are browned, 2 to 3 minutes.

5. Flip the burgers over and sear on the other side, 2 to 3 minutes.

6. Top each burger with a slice of cheese. Cook until the burgers are cooked through and the cheese has melted, 3 to 5 minutes.

7. Remove the burgers from the pan, place them on a plate, and tent with aluminum foil to keep them warm.

8. Spread the butter on the cut sides of the buns. Place them in a large skillet and toast until just browned, 1 to 2 minutes.

9. Spread the Spicy Mayo over the cut sides of the buns, assemble the burgers with the patties and bacon, and serve.

Whole Branzino

Cooking a whole fish in the oven is all about proper technique and patience. But don't let yourself be intimidated: the high fat content of branzino, which is often called "fatty bass," provides a lot of leeway.

1½ lb. whole branzino

2 fresh basil leaves

1 tablespoon kosher salt

1 tablespoon black pepper

2 tablespoons extra-virgin olive oil

½ lemon

1. Preheat the oven to 425°F. Clean the fish, remove the bones, and descale it. Pat it dry with paper towels and rub the flesh with the basil leaves. Season with the salt and pepper and close the fish back up.

2. Place the olive oil in a large cast-iron skillet and warm it over high heat. Place the fish in the pan and cook until it is browned on both sides, 8 to 10 minutes.

3. Place the pan in the oven and roast the fish until the internal temperature is 145°F, about 10 minutes.

4. Remove from the oven and transfer the branzino to a large platter. Squeeze the lemon over the top and enjoy.

Whole Branzino
see page 129

Chicken Tagine

Should you find that the flavor of this tagine is not quite hitting the mark for you, try incorporating a little bit of saffron and/or turmeric.

2 tablespoons extra-virgin olive oil

8 bone-in, skin-on chicken drumsticks or thighs

Salt and pepper, to taste

1 onion, minced

4 garlic cloves, minced

1 teaspoon grated fresh ginger

Zest of 1 lemon

1 teaspoon paprika

½ teaspoon cumin

⅛ teaspoon cayenne pepper

½ teaspoon coriander

¼ teaspoon cinnamon

½ cup white wine

2 cups Chicken Stock (see page 212)

1 carrot, peeled and cut into thin half-moons

1 tablespoon honey

¾ cup halved dried apricots

1 (14 oz.) can of chickpeas, drained and rinsed

Fresh mint, chopped, for garnish

Pearl couscous, cooked, for serving

1. Place the olive oil in a cast-iron Dutch oven and warm it over medium-high heat. Season the chicken with salt and pepper, add it to the pot, and cook, stirring occasionally, until it has browned, about 6 minutes. Remove the chicken from the pot and set it aside.

2. Reduce the heat to medium, add the onion, and cook, stirring occasionally, until it has softened, about 5 minutes. Add the garlic, ginger, lemon zest, paprika, cumin, cayenne, coriander, and cinnamon and cook, stirring continually, for 1 minute.

3. Add the white wine and cook until the alcohol has been cooked off, about 3 minutes, scraping up any browned bits from the bottom of the pot.

4. Add the stock, carrot, honey, and apricots and bring the mixture to a simmer. Nestle the chicken into the mixture and cook until it is cooked through (internal temperature of 165°F), about 10 minutes.

5. Add the chickpeas, cover the pot, and cook until they are heated through, about 5 minutes.

6. Garnish the tagine with mint and serve it with couscous.

Rosemary-Brined Pork Chops with Apples, Potatoes & Brandy

Erin French: "This dish is inspired by my favorite way to cook venison, but uses pork instead—which is most likely much easier to come by in your neck of the woods. It also represents all the flavors that I smell in the air come hunting season."

Basic Brine (see page 241), made with 4 sprigs of fresh rosemary

4 bone-in pork chops (each about 1½ inches thick)

1 lb. baby potatoes

Salt and pepper, to taste

6 tablespoons extra-virgin olive oil

4 tablespoons unsalted butter

2 sprigs of fresh rosemary, needles finely chopped

2 large shallots, sliced lengthwise

2 crisp apples, peeled, quartered, and cored

¼ cup Calvados or other good apple brandy

1. Submerge the pork chips in the cooled brine, cover, and refrigerate for at least 24 and up to 36 hours.

2. When you're ready to cook the pork chops, preheat the oven to 425°F. Put the potatoes in a medium pot and add just enough cold water to cover. Season with salt and bring to a boil, then reduce the heat and simmer the potatoes until just fork-tender, 15 to 20 minutes.

3. Meanwhile, in a small cast-iron skillet over medium-high heat, combine 2 tablespoons of the olive oil, 2 tablespoons of the butter, and the copped rosemary. Once the butter has melted, add the shallots and cook until softened, 8 to 10 minutes. Add the apples and cook for 5 minutes, stirring occasionally.

4. Add the Calvados, stir, and cook for another minute. Reduce the heat to low, add the remaining 2 tablespoons butter, and cook until the apples are just tender, about 5 more minutes. Drain the potatoes and toss with the apple mixture.

5. Heat 2 large cast-iron skillets over high heat with 2 tablespoons of olive oil in each. Remove the pork chops from the brine and pat them dry with paper towels. When the oil shimmers, carefully add the chops to the pans and sear until golden, about 2 minutes. Flip and cook for another 2 minutes. Transfer the pans to the oven and roast until the pork is medium, which will register at 140°F to 145°F on a meat thermometer. Depending on how thick your chops are, this could take 5 to 10 minutes. Allow the chops to rest on a warm plate for 5 minutes before serving. Serve the pork chops with the warm potatoes and apples.

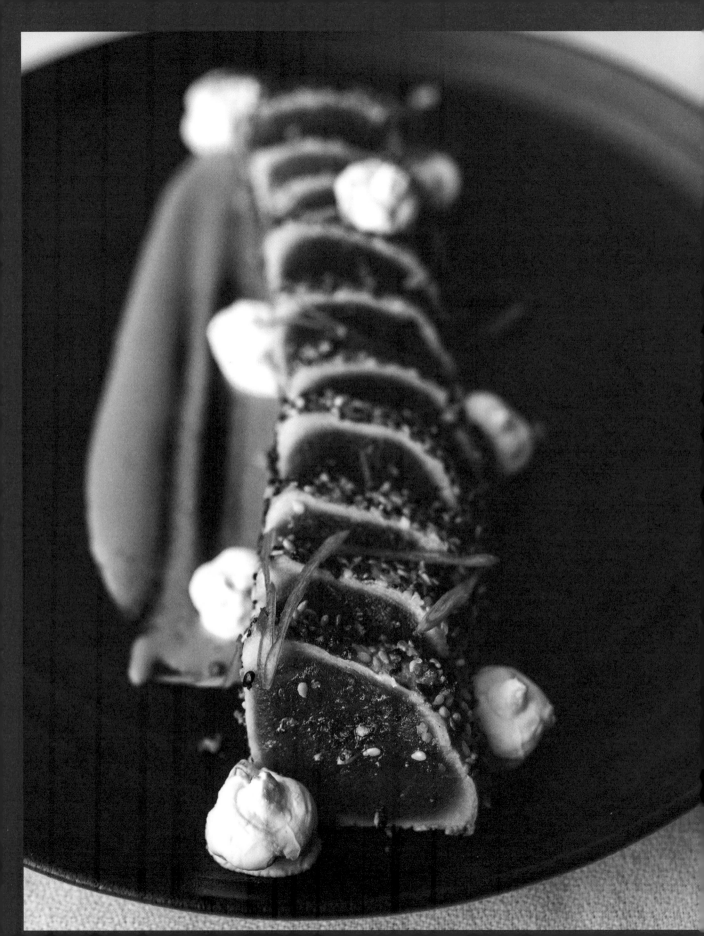

YIELD: *2 Servings* / ACTIVE TIME: 20 Minutes / TOTAL TIME: 30 Minutes

Everything Spice Tuna with Scallion Cream Cheese

The key to working with tuna is getting the sear just right and using a very sharp knife to cut it—do both, and the presentation will be unparalleled.

FOR THE SCALLION PUREE

Salt, to taste

½ lb. scallions, trimmed

1 garlic clove, sliced

1 lemon peel

¼ cup canola oil

FOR THE TUNA

¾ tablespoon garlic flakes

1 tablespoon onion flakes

1½ teaspoons white sesame seeds

1½ teaspoons black sesame seeds

1½ teaspoons poppy seeds

½ lb. tuna steaks

Salt and white pepper, to taste

2 tablespoons canola oil

Scallion Cream Cheese (see page 224), for garnish

1. To begin preparations for the scallion puree, bring water to a boil in a medium saucepan and prepare an ice bath. Add salt and the scallions, garlic, and lemon peel and cook for 2 minutes. Remove the mixture with a strainer and plunge it into the ice bath. Drain the mixture and squeeze it to remove excess moisture.

2. Place the mixture in a blender and puree until smooth. With the blender running, slowly stream in the canola oil until it has emulsified. Taste the puree, adjust the seasoning as necessary, and set the puree aside.

3. To begin preparations for the tuna, place the garlic flakes, onion flakes, sesame seeds, and poppy seeds on a plate and stir to combine.

4. Season the tuna with salt and white pepper and roll it in the seed mixture.

5. Place the canola oil in a large cast-iron skillet and warm it over high heat. Add the tuna and sear it for just 10 seconds on each side.

6. Remove the tuna from the pan and slice it.

7. To serve, spread the scallion puree over the plates, arrange some tuna beside it, and top with dollops of the Scallion Cream Cheese.

YIELD: 2 to 4 Servings / **ACTIVE TIME:** 10 Minutes / **TOTAL TIME:** 1 Hour and 30 Minutes

Pan-Seared Scallops with Marinated Radishes & Pickled Kumquats

Pat the scallops dry before searing and ensure that you do not crowd the pan with too many of them, as this will prevent the scallops from getting a nice, golden brown crust.

2 watermelon radishes, trimmed and diced

½ cup extra-virgin olive oil

¼ cup honey

2 teaspoons rice vinegar

2 teaspoons soy sauce

1 teaspoon sesame oil

1 teaspoon grated fresh ginger

2 teaspoons minced shallot

1 lb. fresh scallops

Salt and white pepper, to taste

3 tablespoons canola oil

2 tablespoons unsalted butter

Pickled Kumquats (see page 229), for garnish

Scallions, chopped, for garnish

Black sesame seeds, toasted, for garnish

1. Place the radishes in a bowl. Place the olive oil, honey, vinegar, soy sauce, sesame oil, ginger, and shallot in a separate bowl and whisk to combine. Pour the mixture over the radishes and let them marinate for 45 minutes.

2. Pat the scallops dry with paper towels and season them with salt and white pepper. Place the canola oil in a large cast-iron skillet and warm it over high heat.

3. Taking care not to crowd the pan, add the scallops and sear until golden brown on the bottom, 1 to 2 minutes.

4. Turn the scallops over, add the butter, and cook the scallops, frequently basting them with the butter, until their interior temperature is 125ºF.

5. Transfer the scallops to a paper towel–lined plate and let them drain briefly.

6. Serve the scallops with the radishes and garnish with the Pickled Kumquats, scallions, and black sesame seeds.

4 bone-in, skin-on chicken thighs

1 tablespoon white vinegar

2 tablespoons fresh lemon juice

6 tablespoons Epis (see page 217)

2 teaspoons adobo seasoning

½ teaspoon black pepper

2 teaspoons garlic powder

Juice of ½ lime

2 tablespoons canola oil

1½ tablespoons tomato paste

1 red bell pepper, stem and seeds removed, sliced

1 green bell pepper, stem and seeds removed, sliced

1 small onion, sliced

6 sprigs of fresh parsley

6 sprigs of fresh thyme

8 whole cloves

1 habanero chile pepper

1 chicken bouillon cube, crushed

Salt, to taste

White rice, for serving

Poule Nan Sos

So many flavors are developed through the process of making this dish that what is at heart a simple stewed chicken becomes staggeringly bold and complex.

---

1. Remove the skin from the chicken and score the meat with a paring knife, cutting to the bone to allow the marinade to work itself into the meat. Place the chicken in a bowl, add the vinegar and lemon juice, and rub them into the chicken. Drain the chicken, place it back in the bowl, and add ¼ cup of the Epis. Toss until the chicken is completely coated, cover the bowl with plastic wrap, and let the chicken marinate in the refrigerator overnight.

2. Place the chicken in a cast-iron Dutch oven and season it with the adobo, black pepper, garlic powder, and lime juice, and stir until well combined. Cover the pot and place it over medium heat. Cook the chicken, turning it every 4 minutes, until it is cooked through, 15 to 20 minutes.

3. Remove the chicken from the pot and place it on a paper towel–lined plate to drain. Pour the pan juices into a bowl and set them aside.

4. Place the Dutch oven over medium-high heat and wait until any residual liquid has evaporated. Add the canola oil and warm it. Pat the chicken dry and carefully place it in the pot. Sear the chicken until browned all over.

5. Add the tomato paste and remaining Epis to the pot and cook, stirring continually, for 1 to 2 minutes.

6. Add half of the bell peppers and the onion to the pot and cook for 1 minute. Stir the reserved pan juices into the pot.

7. Tie the parsley and thyme together with kitchen twine. Poke the cloves into the habanero. Add the herbs, habanero, and bouillon cube to the pot and stir until well combined.

8. Taste the broth and adjust the seasoning as necessary.

9. Reduce the heat to medium-low and cook for 4 to 5 minutes. Taste and adjust the seasoning as necessary.

10. Stir in the remaining peppers and cook, stirring occasionally, until the chicken is very tender, 20 to 25 minutes. Take care not to pierce the habanero when stirring.

11. Taste and season the stew with salt. Ladle the stew over rice and serve.

NY Strip with Arugula Chimichurri

Though most insist that a steak must be cooked over an open fire, the crust that is achieved by searing it in a cast-iron pan is tough to beat.

---

1 lb. NY strip steaks

Salt and pepper, to taste

2 tablespoons extra-virgin olive oil

2 tablespoons unsalted butter

2 sprigs of fresh thyme

2 garlic cloves, smashed

1 shallot, halved

Arugula Chimichurri (see page 232)

Baby arugula, for garnish

1. Preheat the oven to 475°F. Place the steaks on a paper towel–lined plate, season them with salt, and let them sit at room temperature. Pat the steaks occasionally with paper towels to remove the moisture that pools on top.

2. Warm a large cast-iron skillet over high heat. Place the olive oil in the pan, season the steaks with pepper, and place them in the pan.

3. Sear the steaks for 1 minute on each side. Add the butter, thyme, garlic, and shallot and use a large spoon to baste the steaks with the butter for 1 minute.

4. Transfer the steaks to the oven and roast until they are medium-rare (their interiors are 125°F), about 3 minutes. Remove the steaks from the oven and let them rest for 5 minutes.

5. Slice the steaks and season them with salt. Drizzle the chimichurri over the steaks, garnish with arugula, and serve.

FOR THE OCTOPUS

8 cups water

3 oranges, halved

3 limes, halved

½ bunch of fresh parsley

2 shallots, chopped

5 garlic cloves, smashed

2 tablespoons coriander seeds

1 tablespoon black peppercorns

5 lb. octopus

FOR THE SCALLION MAYO

½ cup mayonnaise

1 teaspoon fresh lime juice

1 tablespoon sliced scallion greens

1 tablespoon chopped fresh parsley

Canola oil, as needed

12 Corn Tortillas (see page 214)

Salt and pepper, to taste

Paprika, to taste

1 cup Red Chermoula Sauce
(see page 230)

Fresh cilantro, topped, for garnish

Pickled Carrots (see page 216),
for garnish

1 cup crumbled cotija cheese,
for garnish

Octopus Tostadas

Tacos are too powerful a culinary force to restrict to one day of the week. The tostada is an open-faced taco that was created as a way to use up stale tortillas, and its crunch is welcome in this bright and fresh iteration.

---

1. To prepare the octopus, place all of the ingredients, except for the octopus, in a large pot and bring to a boil. Carefully lower the octopus in the pot and reduce to a simmer. Cook until the tentacles are tender, about 1½ hours.

2. Prepare an ice bath and place the octopus in it.

3. To prepare the scallion mayo, place all of the ingredients in a bowl, stir to combine, and set it aside.

4. Add canola oil to a large, deep cast-iron skillet until it is about 1 inch deep and warm it to 350°F. Add the tortillas to the hot oil one at a time and fry until they are crispy, 1 to 2 minutes. Remove the tostadas from the oven, transfer them to a paper towel–lined plate to drain and season them with salt and paprika. Keep the oil at 350ºF.

5. Remove the octopus from the ice bath, remove the tentacles, and pat them completely dry with paper towels. Add the tentacles one at a time to the hot oil and fry until they are crispy, 2 to 3 minutes. Transfer the fried tentacles to a paper towel–lined plate, let them drain, and season with salt and pepper.

6. When the tentacles are cool enough to handle, cut them into bite-size pieces.

7. Spread the mayo over the tostadas and top them with octopus. Drizzle the chermoula over the top and garnish with cilantro, the Pickled Carrots, and cotija.

Griot

Any real discussion of Haitian cuisine has to include griot, a fried pork dish that is a fixture at parties and festive family dinners.

---

2 lbs. pork shoulder, cubed

¼ cup Epis (see page 217)

2 tablespoons sour orange juice

2 tablespoons fresh lime juice

1½ tablespoons adobo seasoning

1½ tablespoons garlic powder

2 teaspoons sazón

Salt, to taste

6 sprigs of fresh parsley

6 sprigs of fresh thyme

8 whole cloves

1 habanero chile pepper

Canola oil, as needed

Bell peppers, chopped, for garnish

Red onion, chopped, for garnish

Shallots, chopped, for garnish

Fresh herbs, chopped, for garnish

Lime wedges, for serving

1. Place the pork, Epis, juices, adobo, garlic powder, and sazon in a bowl, season with salt, and toss to combine. Cover the bowl and let the pork marinate in the refrigerator for 6 to 7 hours.

2. Place the pork and marinade in a cast-iron Dutch oven and add water until the pork is covered.

3. Tie the parsley and thyme with kitchen twine and add the bouquet garni to the pot. Poke the cloves into the habanero, add it to the pot, and bring to a boil.

4. Reduce the heat to medium and simmer the pork for 20 minutes.

5. Taste the liquid and adjust the seasoning as necessary. Cook until the pork is tender. Using a slotted spoon, transfer the pork to a paper towel–lined plate and let it drain.

6. Add canola oil to a large, deep cast-iron skillet until it is about 1 inch deep and warm it to 350ºF. Working in batches to avoid crowding the pan, add the pork and fry until it is crispy.

7. Transfer the fried griot to another paper towel–lined plate to drain.

8. Garnish the griot with peppers, onion, shallots, and fresh herbs and serve with lime wedges.

YIELD: *2 Servings* / **ACTIVE TIME:** *30 Minutes* / **TOTAL TIME:** *1 Hour*

Roasted King Trumpet Mushrooms with Parsnips, Spinach & Brussels Sprouts

This hearty vegetarian main is guaranteed to be a hit once the weather turns cooler.

---

1 cup chopped parsnips

2 tablespoons extra-virgin olive oil

Salt and pepper, to taste

5 tablespoons canola oil

5 large king trumpet mushrooms, stems removed, halved and scored

4 teaspoons sherry vinegar

2 cups shiitake mushrooms, sliced

2 garlic cloves, minced

2 tablespoons minced shallot

1 tablespoon unsalted butter

2 cups spinach

1 cup Brussels sprout leaves

2 tablespoons chopped fresh parsley

1. Preheat the oven to 400°F. Place the parsnips in a mixing bowl, add the olive oil, season with salt and pepper, and toss to combine. Place the parsnips on a baking sheet and place them in the oven.

2. Roast the parsnips until tender, 10 to 15 minutes. Remove the parsnips from the oven and set them aside. Leave the oven on.

3. Place 3 tablespoons of the canola oil in a large cast-iron skillet and warm it over medium-high heat. Season the king trumpet mushrooms with salt and pepper and place them in the pan, cut side down. Cook until the edges begin to brown, and then place the pan in the oven. Roast the mushrooms until tender, 5 to 8 minutes.

4. Remove the mushrooms from the oven and add half of the vinegar. Toss to coat the mushrooms and place them on a paper towel–lined plate to drain.

5. Place the remaining canola oil in a large skillet and warm it over medium-high heat. Add the shiitake mushrooms, season with salt and pepper, and cook until they are golden brown and crispy, about 8 minutes, stirring occasionally. Add the garlic and shallot and cook, stirring continually, for 1 minute.

6. Add the butter and stir until the mushrooms are coated. Deglaze the pan with the remaining vinegar, scraping any browned bits up from the bottom.

7. Add the spinach, Brussels sprout leaves, and roasted parsnips and season with salt and pepper. Cook until the spinach and Brussels sprout leaves have wilted. Add the parsley and stir to combine.

Harissa Chicken with Pickled Red Onion

Save this one for those moments when you have some time before you'll be called on to serve the dish, but are short on attention to devote to preparing something memorable, as the more time you have to let the chicken marinate in the bold Harissa, the better.

1 lb. skin-on boneless chicken breasts

½ cup Harissa (see page 218)

1½ tablespoons canola oil

Salt and pepper, to taste

2 tablespoons extra-virgin olive oil

2 tablespoons minced shallot

1 garlic clove, minced

¼ cup Chicken Stock (see page 212)

2 teaspoons fresh lime juice

3 tablespoons unsalted butter, cubed

Pickled Red Onion (see page 219), for garnish

1. Rub the chicken breasts with 2 tablespoons of the Harissa. Place them in a bowl and let them marinate in the refrigerator for 2 hours.

2. Preheat the oven to 350°F.

3. Place the canola oil in a large cast-iron skillet and warm it over medium-high heat. Season the chicken with salt and pepper and place it in the pan, skin side down. Place the chicken in the oven and roast until the skin is crispy, 8 to 10 minutes.

4. Turn the chicken over and roast until the internal temperature is 165°F, 10 to 15 minutes.

5. While the chicken is in the oven, place the olive oil in a large skillet and warm it over medium heat. Add the shallot and garlic and cook, stirring frequently, until the shallot is translucent, about 3 minutes.

6. Stir in the remaining Harissa, stock, and lime juice and bring to a boil. Reduce the heat, gradually add the butter, and whisk to emulsify.

7. Remove the pan from heat, taste the sauce, and adjust the seasoning as necessary. Set the sauce aside.

8. Remove the chicken from the oven and let it rest for 5 minutes.

9. Ladle the sauce onto the serving plates. Slice the chicken and place it on top of the sauce. Garnish with Pickled Red Onion and enjoy.

Artichoke à la Barigoule

Typically made with whole peeled artichokes, this classic Provençal preparation is more refined, and can be enjoyed on its own or beside fish or poultry.

2 cups baby artichokes in olive oil, drained and quartered, oil reserved

½ lb. button mushrooms, sliced thin

1 leek, trimmed, halved, rinsed well, and sliced thin

1 garlic clove, minced

2 anchovies in olive oil, drained and finely chopped

½ teaspoon fresh thyme

2 tablespoons all-purpose flour

¼ cup dry vermouth

4 cups Chicken Stock (see page 212), plus more as needed

½ cup peeled and chopped celeriac

1 bay leaf

½ cup heavy cream

1½ tablespoons chopped fresh tarragon

1 teaspoon champagne vinegar

Salt and pepper, to taste

1. Place 2 tablespoons of the olive oil reserved from the artichokes in a cast-iron Dutch oven and warm it over medium heat. Add the artichokes and cook, stirring occasionally, until they are lightly caramelized, about 5 minutes. Remove the pot from heat, transfer the artichokes to a plate, and let them cool.

2. Place the pot back over medium heat and add the mushrooms. Cover the pot and cook for 5 minutes. Remove the cover and cook until most of the liquid the mushrooms release has evaporated, about 5 minutes.

3. Add another tablespoon of the reserved oil and the leek and cook, stirring occasionally, until it has softened, about 5 minutes. Stir in the garlic, anchovies, and thyme and cook, stirring continually, for 1 minute.

4. Stir in the flour, cook for 1 minute, and then add the vermouth. Cook until the alcohol has been cooked off, 1 to 2 minutes.

5. While whisking, gradually add the Chicken Stock. When all of the stock has been incorporated, add the celeriac and bay leaf along with the artichokes and bring the mixture to a boil. Reduce the heat and simmer until the celeriac is tender, 10 to 15 minutes, adding more stock if the level of liquid starts to look a bit too low.

6. Remove the pot from heat, remove the bay leaf, and discard it. Stir in the cream, tarragon, and vinegar, season the soup with salt and pepper, ladle it into warmed bowls, and enjoy.

Lamb Sharba

If lamb is not your thing, this Libyan delicacy can also be made with chicken or fish serving as the protein.

2 tablespoons extra-virgin olive oil

¾ lb. boneless leg of lamb, cut into 1-inch cubes

1 onion, chopped

1 tomato, quartered, seeds removed, sliced thin

1 garlic clove, minced

1 tablespoon tomato paste

1 bunch of fresh mint, tied with twine, plus more for garnish

2 cinnamon sticks

1¼ teaspoons turmeric

1¼ teaspoons paprika

½ teaspoon cumin

8 cups Chicken Stock (see page 212)

1 (14 oz.) can of chickpeas, drained and rinsed

¾ cup orzo

Salt and pepper, to taste

1. Place the olive oil in a cast-iron Dutch oven and warm it over medium-high heat. Add the lamb and cook, turning it as necessary, until it is browned all over, about 5 minutes. Remove the lamb with a slotted spoon and place it on a paper towel–lined plate.

2. Add the onion to the pot and cook, stirring occasionally, until it starts to soften, about 5 minutes. Add the tomato, garlic, tomato paste, mint, cinnamon sticks, turmeric, paprika, and cumin and cook, stirring continually, for 1 minute.

3. Add the stock and bring the mixture to a boil. Return the seared lamb to the pot, reduce the heat, and simmer until the lamb is tender, about 30 minutes.

4. Add the chickpeas and orzo and cook until the orzo is tender, about 10 minutes.

5. Remove the mint and discard it. Season the soup with salt and pepper and ladle it into warmed bowls. Garnish with additional mint and enjoy.

YIELD: 4 Servings / ACTIVE TIME: 15 Minutes / TOTAL TIME: 45 Minutes

Toasted Pasta with Crab

Giving the pasta a deep toasting in a cast-iron skillet lends this dish an authentic Spanish flavor.

¼ cup extra-virgin olive oil

½ lb. angel hair pasta, broken into 2-inch pieces

1 onion, chopped

3 garlic cloves, minced

¼ cup white wine

4 cups Chicken Stock (see page 212)

1 bay leaf

1 (14 oz.) can of diced tomatoes, drained

1 teaspoon paprika

Salt and pepper, to taste

1 lb. lump crabmeat

Fresh parsley, chopped, for garnish

1. Preheat the oven to 425°F. Place 1 tablespoon of the olive oil and the pasta in a large cast-iron skillet and toast the pasta over medium-high heat until it is browned, about 8 minutes. Transfer the pasta to a bowl.

2. Wipe out the skillet, add the remaining olive oil, and warm it over medium heat. Add the onion and cook, stirring occasionally, until it has softened, about 5 minutes. Add the garlic and cook, stirring continually, for 1 minute.

3. Add the wine and cook until the alcohol has been cooked off, 2 to 3 minutes. Add the stock, bay leaf, tomatoes, and paprika and bring the mixture to a boil. Reduce the heat, add the pasta, and simmer until the pasta is tender, about 10 minutes.

4. Season the dish with salt and pepper, add the crab, place the pan in the oven, and bake until the pasta is crispy, about 5 minutes.

5. Remove the pan from the oven, garnish the dish with parsley, and enjoy.

THE CAST IRON / 156

'Nduja Shakshuka

'Nduja, the famed chile paste from Calabria, elevates what is already the best option when you're having breakfast for dinner.

2 tablespoons extra-virgin olive oil

1 onion, chopped

2 green bell peppers, stems and seeds removed, chopped

2 garlic cloves, minced

2 tablespoons 'nduja

1 teaspoon coriander

1 teaspoon sweet paprika

½ teaspoon cumin

1 teaspoon turmeric

Pinch of red pepper flakes

2 tablespoons tomato paste

5 ripe tomatoes, chopped

Salt and pepper, to taste

6 eggs

1 cup crumbled feta cheese

¼ cup chopped fresh parsley, for garnish

¼ cup chopped fresh mint, for garnish

1. Place the olive oil in a large cast-iron skillet and warm it over medium heat. Add the onion and cook, stirring occasionally, until it has softened, about 5 minutes. Add the bell peppers and cook, stirring occasionally, until they have softened, about 5 minutes.

2. Add the garlic, 'nduja, coriander, paprika, cumin, turmeric, red pepper flakes, and tomato paste and cook, stirring continually, for 1 minute. Add the tomatoes and bring the mixture to a boil. Reduce the heat, cover the pan, and simmer for 15 minutes.

3. Remove the cover and cook until the shakshuka has reduced slightly, about 5 minutes.

4. Season the shakshuka with salt and pepper. Using the back of a wooden spoon, make six wells in the mixture. Crack an egg into each well and sprinkle the feta over the dish.

5. Reduce the heat to a simmer, cover the pan, and cook until the egg whites are set, 6 to 8 minutes.

6. Remove the pan from heat, garnish with the parsley and mint, and enjoy.

Ratatouille with Poached Eggs

If you are someone who loves nothing more than spending a summer day in the garden, this simple, beautiful dish allows you to make the most of your labors.

¼ cup extra-virgin olive oil

1 cup chopped onion

4 garlic cloves, minced

2 tablespoons tomato paste

1 cup chopped red bell pepper

1 cup chopped yellow bell pepper

1 cup chopped zucchini

½ cup water

2 tablespoons herbes de Provence

Salt and pepper, to taste

6 eggs

¼ cup fresh basil leaves

½ cup shaved Parmesan cheese

1. Place the olive oil in a cast-iron Dutch oven and warm it over medium heat. Add the onion and cook, stirring occasionally, until it has softened, about 5 minutes. Add the garlic and tomato paste and cook, stirring continually, for 1 minute.

2. Add the bell peppers and cook, stirring occasionally, until they have softened, about 5 minutes.

3. Add the zucchini, water, and herbes de Provence, cover the pot, and cook for 10 minutes. Remove the cover and cook until the liquid has reduced, about 5 minutes.

4. Season the ratatouille with salt and pepper. Using the back of a wooden spoon, make six wells in the ratatouille. Gently crack an egg into each well, reduce the heat so that the ratatouille simmers, and cover the pot. Cook until the egg whites are set, 6 to 8 minutes.

5. Spoon the ratatouille and poached eggs into bowls, garnish each portion with the basil and Parmesan, and enjoy.

¼ cup extra-virgin olive oil

1 cup chopped onions

½ teaspoon kosher salt

1 garlic clove, minced

2 teaspoons grated fresh ginger

¼ teaspoon turmeric

½ teaspoon paprika

2 cups water

1 lb. boneless, skinless chicken thighs, cut into ½-inch-wide strips

4 eggs, beaten

2 tablespoons chopped fresh cilantro

2 tablespoons chopped fresh parsley

¾ cup slivered almonds, toasted

2 tablespoons confectioners' sugar

2 teaspoons cinnamon

½ lb. frozen phyllo dough, thawed

YIELD: 4 to 6 Servings / **ACTIVE TIME:** 1 Hour / **TOTAL TIME:** 2 Hours and 30 Minutes

Chicken B'stilla

Morocco's take on chicken pot pie is sure to become your favorite spin on the comforting classic.

---

1. Place 1 tablespoon of the olive oil in a medium sauce-pan and warm it over medium heat. Add the onions and salt and cook, stirring occasionally, until the onions start to soften, about 5 minutes.

2. Add the garlic, ginger, turmeric, and paprika and cook, stirring continually, until fragrant, about 1 minute. Add the water and bring the mixture to a boil.

3. Reduce the heat so that the mixture simmers and add the chicken. Cook until the chicken can be shredded, about 15 minutes. Remove the chicken, shred it, and let it cool.

4. Reduce the heat to low, add the eggs in a slow drizzle, and cook until they are just set, 2 to 3 minutes.

5. Remove the pan from heat, fold in the shredded chicken, cilantro, and parsley, and let the mixture cool.

6. Preheat the oven to 375°F. Place the almonds, 1½ tablespoons of the confectioners' sugar, and half of the cinnamon in a bowl and stir until combined.

7. Brush a medium cast-iron skillet with some of the remaining olive oil. Lay 1 sheet of the phyllo in the pan, let-

ting it hang over the sides, and brush it with olive oil. Lay another sheet on top, 2 inches to the right of where you laid the first one. Brush it with olive oil and repeat with 8 more sheets of phyllo. Make sure to keep any sheets of phyllo that you are not working with covered so that they do not dry out.

8. Spread the almond mixture over the last layer of phyllo. Pour the chicken mixture on top of that and use a rubber spatula to spread it into an even layer.

9. Place a piece of parchment paper on a work surface. Place a sheet of phyllo in the center of the parchment and brush it with olive oil. Repeat with 3 more sheets of phyllo dough. After brushing the top sheet with olive oil, fold the stack of phyllo like a book.

10. Lay this stack of phyllo on top of the filling and fold any overhanging phyllo over the top. Combine the remaining confectioners' sugar and cinnamon and sprinkle this mixture over the phyllo.

11. Place the pan in the oven and bake until the b'stilla is crispy and golden brown, about 40 minutes. Remove the b'stilla from the oven and let it cool briefly before serving.

YIELD: 4 Servings / ACTIVE TIME: 30 Minutes / TOTAL TIME: 30 Minutes

Boiled Beef Dinner

This recipe comes courtesy of the great chef and writer Gabrielle Hamilton, who puts her inimitable spin on a comforting classic.

---

8 cups Beef Stock (see page 211), made with oxtail

1½ lbs. trimmed beef tenderloin, cut into 4 portions at 6 oz. each

4 small sheets of caul fat

4 oz. veal heart, thinly sliced

4 oz. cooked veal tongue, cut into ¼-inch slices across the tongue

4 veal marrow bones, cut into 1-inch pieces

8 carrots, peeled

12 pearl onions, blanched and peeled

8 baby turnips, peeled

2 lbs. oxtail, browned, braised, and picked over—bones and cartilage discarded

4 leeks, split lengthwise and soaked in clean water to remove any lingering sand

1 cup peas

4 small stems of fresh thyme, leaves stripped, stems discarded

Fresh horseradish root, to taste

Salt and pepper, to taste

Grey sea salt, for topping

1. Place the stock in a cast-iron Dutch oven and bring it to a simmer over medium heat.

2. Season beef tenderloin on both sides with salt and pepper and a few leaves of fresh thyme and wrap each in a small sheet of caul fat, creating neat bundles. Add beef tenderloin and marrow bones to simmering broth and let it cook for 2 minutes. Add onions, carrots, and turnips to the simmering broth. Add the oxtail meat to the simmering broth. Add the leeks to the simmering broth and continue cooking it for 4 minutes. Add peas, sliced tongue, and veal heart and cook for 1 minute.

3. The beef tenderloin takes about 15 minutes to cook from its raw state to a perfect medium rare. The rest of the ingredients have different cooking times; add them in stages from longest cooking to shortest cooking, ending with the peas, so that when the tenderloin is finished, so is everything else, and the finished dish is ready to be served with all the ingredients accurately cooked.

4. Place the meats and vegetables with care and grace in the large bowls and ladle the broth around evenly. Reserve the rest of the broth for the next batch. Season with a few grains of grey sea salt. Grate a light dusting of fresh horseradish over each bowl and serve.

Pan-Roasted Monkfish with Braised Fennel

A beautifully balanced dish that targets every single tastebud, and is made effortless with the unsurpassed heat-conducting abilities of cast iron.

---

6 tablespoons extra-virgin olive oil

1 tablespoon dried oregano

2 tablespoons red wine vinegar

½ onion, finely diced

2 teaspoons Dijon mustard

2 tablespoons minced Kalamata olives

2 tablespoons minced green olives

1 tablespoon minced capers

1 tablespoon chopped fresh parsley

Salt and pepper, to taste

1½ lbs. monkfish fillets, cut into 2-inch cubes

Pine nuts, toasted and chopped, for garnish

Parmesan cheese, shaved, for garnish

Braised Fennel (see page 222), for serving

Lemon wedges, for serving

1. Place ¼ cup of the olive oil in a small saucepan and warm it over low heat. Add the oregano, remove the pan from heat, and cover it. Let the oil steep for 5 minutes.

2. Add the vinegar, onion, mustard, olives, capers, and parsley, season the relish with salt and pepper, and stir to combine. Transfer the relish to a bowl and set it aside.

3. Place the remaining olive oil in a large cast-iron skillet and warm it over medium-high heat. Pat the monkfish dry with paper towels and season it with salt and pepper. Place the monkfish in the pan and cook until it is golden brown, 3 to 4 minutes. Turn it over and cook until it is cooked through (internal temperature of 160°F), another 3 to 4 minutes.

4. Transfer the monkfish to a serving platter, garnish it with the pine nuts and Parmesan, and serve with the olive relish, Braised Fennel, and lemon wedges.

Roasted Grapes & Sausage

A simple oven-roasted preparation that features the beautiful contrast of salty, spicy sausage and the heightened sweetness of grapes.

1½ lbs. spicy sausage

1 bunch of muscat grapes

6 oz. fresh mozzarella cheese, torn

2 tablespoons Balsamic Glaze (see page 223)

1. Preheat the oven to 500°F. Cut the sausage into ¼-inch-thick slices, place them in a large cast-iron skillet, and add the grapes. Toss to evenly distribute and place the pan over medium-high heat. Cook, stirring occasionally, until the sausage starts to brown, about 5 minutes.

2. Place the pan in the oven and cook until the sausage is well browned and cooked through and the grapes have collapsed, 15 to 20 minutes.

3. Remove the pan from the oven and transfer the mixture to a serving platter.

4. Sprinkle the mozzarella over the sausage and grapes, drizzle the Balsamic Glaze over the top, and enjoy.

YIELD: 2 Servings / ACTIVE TIME: 30 Minutes / TOTAL TIME: 30 Minutes

Crispy Salmon Rice

Use the largest cast-iron skillet you have in your collection, as the greater the surface area, the better the result.

2 tablespoons avocado oil

½ white onion, minced

¼ cup sliced scallions

¼ cup chopped fresh parsley

2 teaspoons kosher salt

2 cups leftover white rice

6 oz. salmon belly, chopped

1 tablespoon pomegranate molasses

1 tablespoon apple cider vinegar

1. Place the avocado oil in a large cast-iron skillet and warm it over high heat. Add the onion, scallions, parsley, and salt and cook, stirring frequently, until the onion is translucent, about 3 minutes.

2. Add the rice and cook, stirring frequently, until the rice is crispy, 3 to 5 minutes. Add the salmon, reduce the heat to medium-high, and cook until the salmon is cooked through, about 4 minutes.

3. Place the pomegranate molasses and vinegar in a small bowl and whisk to combine. Add this mixture to the pan and stir until incorporated.

4. Remove the pan from heat and enjoy immediately.

Crispy Salmon Rice
see page 169

Short Ribs with Braised Cauliflower & Stuffed Tomatoes

In truth, any of the three components here will make for an outstanding dinner. Together, they are an outright feast.

1. Preheat the oven to 300°F. Place the olive oil in a cast-iron Dutch oven and warm it over medium-high heat. Season the short ribs with salt and pepper, add them to the pot, and sear them for 1 minute on each side. Remove the short ribs from the pot and set them aside.

2. Reduce the heat to medium, add the onion, carrot, and celery, and cook, stirring occasionally, until they have softened, about 5 minutes. Add the garlic, tomato paste, ras el hanout, and thyme and cook, stirring continually, for 1 minute.

3. Add the red wine and cook until the alcohol has been cooked off, about 3 minutes, scraping up any browned bits from the bottom of the pan.

4. Add the prune juice, stock, bay leaf, and prunes and bring the mixture to a boil. Return the short ribs to the pot, cover the pot, and place it in the oven. Braise the short ribs until they are extremely tender, 3 to 4 hours.

5. Remove the pot from the oven, remove the cooked short ribs, bay leaf, and half of the prunes, and set them aside. Transfer the mixture remaining in the Dutch oven to a food processor and blitz until smooth.

6. Return the sauce to the Dutch oven, add the reserved prunes and short ribs, and stir in the vinegar. Bring the dish to a simmer, taste, and adjust the seasoning as necessary.

7. Garnish with cilantro and sesame seeds and serve with the Braised Cauliflower and Couscous-Stuffed Tomatoes.

2 tablespoons extra-virgin olive oil

3 lbs. bone-in short ribs

Salt and pepper, to taste

1 onion, chopped

1 carrot, peeled and chopped

2 celery stalks, chopped

4 garlic cloves, minced

1 tablespoon tomato paste

1 tablespoon ras el hanout

1 teaspoon fresh thyme

½ cup red wine

2 cups prune juice

2 cups Beef Stock (see page 211)

1 bay leaf

1 cup prunes

2 teaspoons red wine vinegar

Fresh cilantro, chopped, for garnish

Sesame seeds, toasted, for garnish

Braised Cauliflower (see page 225), for serving

Couscous-Stuffed Tomatoes (see page 236), for serving

Za'atar Chicken

Struggling to get a chicken to cook evenly when you roast it? Spatch-cocking and a couple of cast-iron skillets are here to save the day.

---

4 lb. whole chicken

2 tablespoons extra-virgin olive oil

2 tablespoons za'atar

Honey-Glazed Carrots (see page 226), for serving

Roasted Root Vegetables (see page 227), for serving

1. Place a wire rack in a rimmed baking sheet. Place the chicken, breast side down, on a cutting board. Using kitchen shears, cut out the chicken's backbone. Flip the chicken over so the breast side is facing up. Push down on the middle of the chicken to flatten it as much as possible. Pat the chicken dry and place it on the wire rack.

2. Place the chicken in the refrigerator and let it rest, uncovered, overnight.

3. Remove the chicken from the refrigerator and let it rest at room temperature.

4. Preheat the oven to 425°F.

5. Place the olive oil in a large cast-iron skillet and warm it over medium heat. Add the chicken to the pan and weigh it down with another cast-iron skillet—this added weight will help the chicken cook evenly. Cook until the chicken is golden brown on each side, 15 to 20 minutes.

6. Place the chicken on a baking sheet, breast side up, sprinkle the za'atar over the chicken, and place it in the oven. Roast the chicken until it is cooked through (internal temperature is 165°F), about 15 minutes.

7. Remove the chicken from the oven and let it rest for 10 minutes. Serve with the glazed carrots and other Roasted Root Vegetables.

As you no doubt already know, cast iron does not beg off when the time comes to soothe a sweet tooth. Well, neither do the world's very best chefs. Filled with recipes that allow you to effortlessly capture the best of each season and provide a memorable meal with the decadent punctuation that it deserves, the inventive recipes in this chapter will not only have you thinking differently about your cast- iron cookware, but about dessert in general.

Rhubarb Spoon Cake

This cake is the pleasant result of one of the rare missteps Erin French experienced in the kitchen: "I added too much butter and not enough flour, and I ended up with a pink and white swirly mess. But something really magical had happened—it tasted like gooey vanilla cake with warmed compote mixed in. Now when I serve this (purposefully), I hand out spoons and we all dig in."

½ cup unsalted butter, melted, plus more as needed

1 cup all-purpose flour, plus more as needed

2 teaspoons baking powder

½ cup sugar

½ teaspoon salt

1 large egg

1 teaspoon pure vanilla extract

½ cup whole milk

¼ cup sour cream

Rhubarb Compote (see page 246)

Perfectly Whipped Cream (see page 247)

1. Preheat the oven to 400°F. Coat a medium cast-iron skillet with butter and flour, shaking out any excess flour.

2. In a medium bowl, combine the flour, baking powder, sugar, and salt. In a large bowl, whisk together the egg, vanilla, milk, sour cream, and melted butter. Gently stir the wet ingredients into the dry until they are just incorporated.

3. Pour about two-thirds of the compote into the greased skillet and spread evenly. Pour the cake batter over it, spread evenly, then dollop the remaining compote over the top. Use a butter knife to swirl together the batter and compote.

4. Bake until a cake tester or knife inserted in the middle of the cake comes out clean, about 25 minutes. Serve warm, directly from the skillet, with a big spoon and a bowl of whipped cream to dollop on top.

Pumpkin Spice Drop Doughnuts

A quick and delicious dessert that was made to feed a big crowd on a crisp fall Saturday.

Canola oil, as needed

2 cups all-purpose flour

⅓ cup brown sugar

2½ teaspoons baking powder

¼ teaspoon fine sea salt

¾ teaspoon cinnamon, plus more for topping

¼ teaspoon freshly grated nutmeg

1 large egg

1 cup canned pumpkin puree

3 tablespoons milk

2 tablespoons unsalted butter, melted

1 teaspoon pure vanilla extract

Sugar, for topping

1. Add canola oil to a cast-iron Dutch oven until it is about 2 inches deep and warm it to 375°F.

2. Place the flour, brown sugar, baking powder, salt, cinnamon, and nutmeg in a large mixing bowl and whisk to combine.

3. Place the egg, pumpkin, and milk in a separate mixing bowl and whisk to combine. Add the butter and vanilla and whisk to incorporate.

4. Add the wet mixture to the dry mixture and stir until it comes together as a smooth dough.

5. Working in batches of 5 or 6, drop teaspoons of the dough into the hot oil. Fry until they doughnuts are golden brown, 3 to 4 minutes, turning them as necessary.

6. Remove the doughnuts from the pot and transfer them to a paper towel–lined plate to drain.

7. Combine cinnamon and sugar in a baking dish, roll the doughnuts in the cinnamon sugar, and enjoy.

YIELD: 1 Cake / **ACTIVE TIME:** 30 Minutes / **TOTAL TIME:** 1 Hour and 30 Minutes

Plum Upside-Down Cake

Sean Brock: "Pineapple upside-down cake is a classic dessert that registers with people no matter where they're from. There is no such thing as homegrown pineapple in the South, of course, so I use gorgeous local black plums. The sweet and tart flavor of a good plum is delicious for the same reason a ripe pineapple tastes good, so using plums for this dessert makes perfect sense."

1. Position a rack in the middle of the oven and preheat the oven to 350°F.

2. For the plum topping: Combine the butter and brown sugar in a 10-inch cast-iron skillet and cook over medium heat, stirring, until the butter melts and the sugar dissolves. Continue to cook until the mixture boils and turns golden brown, about 2 minutes. Stir in the salt, remove from the stove, and cool for 10 minutes.

3. Add the plum quarters to the skillet, arranging them in a pinwheel pattern starting in the center and working your way out to the edges. Set aside while you make the cake batter.

4. For the cake: Sift the flour, baking powder, cinnamon, ginger, and salt into a bowl and set aside.

5. Combine the butter and sugar in the bowl of a stand mixer fitted with the paddle attachment (or use a large bowl and a hand mixer). Split the vanilla bean lengthwise in half and, using the back of a paring knife, scrape out the seeds and add to the butter mixture (reserve the vanilla pod for another use, if desired). Cream the butter and sugar on medium speed, scraping down the sides as necessary, until light and fluffy, about 5 minutes.

Reduce the speed to low and add the dry ingredients alternately with the milk in 3 increments, starting and ending with the dry ingredients and beating until just incorporated, scraping down the sides after each addition. Do not overmix the batter.

6. Using the back of a spoon or an offset spatula, carefully spread the batter in an even layer over the plums, taking care not to disturb the pattern you made. Bake the cake for 30 to 35 minutes, until the top is golden brown, and a cake tester inserted in the center comes out clean; rotate the skillet halfway through baking for even cooking. Remove the cake from the oven and cool in the skillet on a baking rack for 20 minutes.

7. Run a paring knife around the edges of the cake to release it from the skillet and, using pot holders or oven mitts, place a cake plate on top of the skillet, invert the skillet and the plate, and gently lift off the skillet, leaving the cake fruit side up.

8. Slice the cake and serve. Any leftover cake can be tightly covered, once cooled, and refrigerated for up to 1 day. Remove from the refrigerator 30 minutes before serving.

FOR THE TOPPING

3 tablespoons unsalted butter

⅔ cup packed light brown sugar

⅛ teaspoon kosher salt

1 lb. ripe black plums, quartered and pitted

FOR THE CAKE

1⅔ cups all-purpose flour

1½ teaspoons baking powder

½ teaspoon ground cinnamon

¼ teaspoon ground ginger

¼ teaspoon kosher salt

½ cup unsalted butter, diced, at room temperature

¾ cup sugar

½ vanilla bean

¾ cup whole milk

Tequeño

Replacing the traditional cheese filling with mashed plantain is a masterstroke.

---

4 large eggs

¾ cup plus ½ cup water

⅓ cup sugar

2 tablespoons honey

1⅔ cups all-purpose flour

1 teaspoon baking soda

½ teaspoon fine sea salt

Canola oil, as needed

7 oz. plantains, chopped

2 teaspoons cinnamon, plus more for topping

1. Place the eggs, ¾ cup of water, the sugar, and honey in a mixing bowl and stir to combine. Gradually add the flour, baking soda, and salt and stir until the mixture comes together as a smooth dough. Form the dough into a ball, coat a bowl lightly with canola oil, and place the dough in it. Cover the bowl with plastic wrap and let it rest in the refrigerator overnight.

2. Place the plantains, remaining water, and cinnamon in a saucepan and simmer over medium-low heat until the plantains are tender, about 15 minutes. Remove the pan from heat and let the mixture cool for 1½ hours. After 1½ hours, mash the plantains, place them in a piping bag fitted with a fine tip, and set it aside.

3. Remove the dough from the refrigerator and cut it into 20 pieces. Form the pieces into seamless balls, place them on a piece of parchment paper, and let them rest for 30 minutes.

4. Add canola oil to a cast-iron Dutch oven until it is about 2 inches deep and warm it to 375ºF. Poke a hole into the balls of dough and pipe some of the mashed plantains into each one.

5. Working in batches to avoid crowding the pot, gently slip the balls of dough into the hot oil and cook until they are golden brown all over, turning them as necessary. Transfer the fried bread to a paper towel–lined plate and let them drain.

6. Dust the fried bread with cinnamon and enjoy.

YIELD: 8 Servings / ACTIVE TIME: 15 Minutes / TOTAL TIME: 50 Minutes

Strawberry & Gingerbread Dutch Baby

Cultured butter, with its more complex taste and higher fat content, is the secret weapon in this elevated baby.

---

4 eggs

2 tablespoons dark brown sugar

⅔ cup all-purpose flour

¾ teaspoon cinnamon

½ teaspoon grated fresh ginger

½ teaspoon freshly grated nutmeg

¼ teaspoon ground cloves

¼ teaspoon fine sea salt

1 tablespoon Vermont Creamery Vanilla Crème Fraîche, plus more for topping

⅔ cup whole milk

3 tablespoons Vermont Creamery Cultured Butter

1 quart of fresh strawberries, hulled and sliced

⅓ cup sliced almonds

3 fresh basil leaves, sliced thin

1. Preheat the oven to 400°F. Crack the eggs into a food processor and blitz until they are very smooth and pale, about 2 minutes. Add the brown sugar, flour, spices, salt, crème fraîche, and milk and blitz until the mixture is once again very smooth.

2. Place the cultured butter in a large cast-iron skillet and place the pan in the oven until the butter has melted and started to brown, about 5 minutes.

3. Remove the skillet from the oven and swirl the butter to coat the bottom and sides of the pan. Pour the batter into the pan and return it to the oven.

4. Bake for about 7 minutes, remove the pan from the oven, and sprinkle half of the strawberries and almonds over the batter. Return the pan to the oven and bake until the baby has climbed the sides of the pan and the edges are golden brown, 15 to 20 minutes.

5. Remove the baby from the oven and top it with the remaining strawberries and almonds and the basil. Slice and top each serving with additional crème fraîche.

YIELD: 6 Servings / **ACTIVE TIME:** 10 Minutes / **TOTAL TIME:** 1 Hour

Peach & Ginger Cobbler

Erin French: "My grandpa Jack—or Gramps, as we sometimes called him—was a fixture at my dad's diner, always on the line, whistling, flipping eggs. He was also the one to make the dumplings, and he swore by this magical all-purpose baking mix where you just had to add water to make anything—biscuits, pancakes, anything. I've yet to figure out his exact recipe, but in my tinkering I discovered this super simple biscuit recipe to sit atop a cobbler."

FOR THE FILLING

6 ripe but firm peaches

1 tablespoon grated fresh ginger

¼ cup sugar

Zest and juice of 1 lemon

1 teaspoon cornstarch

FOR THE TOPPING

1 cup all-purpose flour

½ cup sugar

1 teaspoon baking powder

½ teaspoon salt

2 teaspoons lemon zest

6 tablespoons unsalted butter, cold, cubed

¼ cup chopped candied ginger

⅓ cup buttermilk, plus more as needed

Sanding sugar, for topping

1. Preheat oven to 425°F.

2. Make the filling: Slice the peaches into wedges and toss them in a medium bowl with ginger, granulated sugar, lemon zest and juice, and cornstarch until well coated. Let the mixture sit for 20 minutes.

3. Meanwhile, make the topping: In a medium bowl, whisk together the flour, granulated sugar, baking powder, salt, and zest. Using a pastry blender, fork, or your fingers, work in the butter until it's in pea-sized pieces. Stir in the candied ginger, then the buttermilk. If the mixture seems too dry to spoon over the fruit, add a bit more buttermilk.

4. Pour the peaches into a large cast-iron skillet.

5. Drop 8 biscuit-sized dollops of the mixture on top of the peaches. Sprinkle sanding sugar over the top and bake until the peaches are tender and bubbly and the topping is golden and cooked through, 25 to 30 minutes. Serve warm.

6 to 8 Honeycrisp apples, peeled, cores removed, quartered

1⅓ cups all-purpose flour, plus more as needed

¼ cup confectioners' sugar

½ teaspoon fine sea salt

½ cup unsalted butter, chilled

1 egg, beaten

6 tablespoons salted butter, softened

⅔ cup sugar

Tarte Tatin

In the late nineteenth century, the Tatin sisters, Caroline and Stephanie, ran the Hotel Tatin in Lamotte-Beuvron, a small town in France's Loire Valley. Stephanie, who was in charge of the kitchen, was renowned for her apple tart. But during one lunch rush she accidently placed it in the oven upside down. She shrugged off the mistake and served it anyway, and word of her wonderful misstep soon reached Paris. There, it quickly ascended onto the menu at the famed restaurant Maxim's, assuring the Tarte Tatin's place in history.

1. Place the apples in a mixing bowl and let them sit in the refrigerator for 48 hours. This will dry the apples out, keeping the amount of liquid to a reasonable level.

2. Whisk together the flour, confectioners' sugar, and salt in a large bowl. Add the unsalted butter and use your fingers or a pastry blender to work the mixture until it is a collection of coarse clumps. Add the egg and work the mixture until the dough just holds together. Shape it into a ball and cover it with plastic wrap. Flatten it into a 4-inch disk and refrigerate for 1 hour. If preparing ahead of time, the dough will keep in the refrigerator overnight.

3. Preheat the oven to 375°F. Coat a 10-inch cast-iron skillet with the salted butter and place the pan over low heat. When the butter is melted, remove the skillet from heat and sprinkle the sugar evenly over the butter. Place the apple slices in a circular pattern, starting at the center of the pan and working out to the edge. The pieces should overlap and face the same direction.

4. Place the dough on a flour-dusted work surface and roll it out to ⅛ inch thick. Use the roller to carefully roll up the dough. Place it over the apples and tuck the dough in around the edges.

5. Place the skillet over low heat and gradually raise it until the juices in the pan are a deep amber color, about 7 minutes.

6. Place the skillet in the oven and bake until the crust is golden brown and firm, 35 to 40 minutes.

7. Remove the tart from the oven, let it cool for about 5 minutes, and then run a knife around the edges to loosen the tart. Using oven mitts, carefully invert the tart onto a large plate. Place any apples that are stuck to the skillet back on the tart and enjoy.

Salted Honey & Apple Cake

Salting the honey adds a shocking amount of complexity to this cake's flavor.

¾ cup all-purpose flour

1 teaspoon baking powder

¾ teaspoon kosher salt

½ teaspoon cinnamon

¼ cup sour cream, plus more for serving

¼ cup avocado oil

2 teaspoons pure vanilla extract

½ cup sugar

2 eggs

1½ teaspoons unsalted butter

¼ cup honey, plus more for serving

1 baking apple, peeled, cored, and sliced into thin rounds

Maldon sea salt, for topping

1. Preheat the oven to 350°F. Place the flour, baking powder, ½ teaspoon of the salt, and the cinnamon in a small bowl and whisk until combined.

2. Place the sour cream, avocado oil, and vanilla in a separate bowl and stir until combined. Place the sugar and eggs in a separate bowl and whisk until the mixture is foamy, about 2 minutes.

3. Add half of the flour mixture to the egg mixture and gently stir to incorporate. Stir in half of the sour cream mixture, add the remaining flour mixture, and stir until incorporated. Add the remaining sour cream mixture and stir until the mixture just comes together. Set the batter aside.

4. Butter the bottom and sides of a small cast-iron skillet and add the honey, swirling the pan to ensure the honey covers as much of the pan as possible. Sprinkle the remaining salt over the honey.

5. Arrange the apple slices on top of the honey, overlapping them to fit the pan. Pour the cake batter over the apple and tap the pan on the counter a few times to remove any large bubbles.

6. Place the cake in the oven and bake until it is golden brown and springs back when gently touched with a finger, about 30 minutes.

7. Remove the cake from the oven and let it cool in the pan for 10 minutes. Run an offset spatula or knife around the pan and invert the cake onto a cooling rack. Let the cake cool for another 20 minutes before transferring to a platter and sprinkling the Maldon sea salt over the top. Serve with additional sour cream and honey.

YIELD: 2 Servings / **ACTIVE TIME:** 25 Minutes / **TOTAL TIME:** 4 to 5 Days

Fermented Banana Fritters

Once you know what warning signs to watch for when fermenting bananas, this recipe becomes a very straightforward process, and an irresistible one.

---

2 bananas

1 teaspoon active dry yeast

2 cups water, plus more as needed

½ cup all-purpose flour

1 teaspoon baking powder

2 tablespoons sugar

1 tablespoon cinnamon

Canola oil, as needed

2 tablespoons peanut butter, for serving

1. Peel the bananas, slice them into ½-inch-thick rounds, and place them in a mason jar. Add the yeast and then cover the bananas with the water. It is important that the bananas are completely covered, so add more water as necessary. Cover the jar and place it in a cupboard, keeping it at roughly 70°F, for 4 to 5 days, until the bananas start to smell a little like alcohol, though not funky. Any bananas at the top that brown should be thrown away.

2. Drain the bananas, place them in a mixing bowl, and mash them. Add the flour and baking powder and stir until well combined.

3. Place the sugar and cinnamon in a bowl and stir to combine.

4. Add canola oil to a large, deep cast-iron skillet until it is about 1 inch deep and warm it to 325°F. Scoop tablespoons of the batter and fry until they are puffy and golden brown on one side, 1½ to 2 minutes. Turn the fritters over and cook until they are puffy and golden brown all over.

5. Remove the fritters from the hot oil, place them in the cinnamon sugar, and toss to coat.

6. Place the peanut butter in a microwave-safe bowl and microwave on medium in 10-second increments until it has liquefied.

7. To serve, spread the melted peanut butter on a small plate and pile the fritters on top.

Caramelized Pear & Cornmeal Skillet Cake

Erin French: "I get a lot of requests to make this cake for special occasions—especially my son's birthday. I think this has to do with how dramatic it is to see the cake flipped from the skillet to reveal the impressive, deeply caramelized amber crown of fanned pear slices. Anyone can pull this off, really. My one recommendation is that you buy good-quality stone-ground cornmeal—not the cheap stuff that tastes like chicken feed."

FOR THE PEARS

5 ripe but firm pears

3 tablespoons unsalted butter

½ cup sugar

FOR THE CAKE

1 cup all-purpose flour

½ cup stone-ground cornmeal

1½ teaspoons baking powder

½ teaspoon salt

½ cup unsalted butter, at room temperature

1 cup sugar

2 large eggs, at room temperature

1 teaspoon pure vanilla extract

½ cup sour cream

1. Caramelize the pears: Peel, halve, and core the pears (a melon baller works well for this last step). Without cutting through the top ½ inch of the pear, slice each half lengthwise four or five times.

2. In a large cast-iron skillet, heat the butter over medium heat until melted. Stir in the sugar. Put one pear half in the center of the pan, domed side down, and arrange the rest of the pear halves in the skillet (also domed sides down) so the slices fan slightly. Let the pears cook, untouched, over medium heat until the sugar has turned a deep, golden caramel color, 15 to 20 minutes. Rotate the skillet if there seem to be any hot spots.

3. Meanwhile, preheat the oven to 350°F. Make the cake batter: Combine the flour, cornmeal, baking powder, and salt in a small bowl.

4. In a stand mixer or medium bowl, beat the butter until light and fluffy. Slowly add the sugar and beat again until light and fluffy. Add the eggs one at a time, mixing after each until well incorporated. Add the vanilla and sour cream. Slowly stir in the dry ingredients until just incorporated.

5. Spread the batter over the pears in the skillet and bake until a tester inserted in the cake comes out clean, about 25 minutes. Let the cake cool for just a few minutes (not too long or the sugar will start to set and the cake will stick to the pan!). Run a knife around the edge of the skillet, top with a large, rimmed plate or platter, and, armed with oven mitts, carefully invert the cake onto the plate. Serve warm.

Sockerkaka

Only cast iron can supply the exterior crumb with the proper burnish. Serve plain, or top slices with sliced citrus, a cinnamon-rich applesauce, or lightly sweetened whipped cream.

---

2 cups all-purpose flour

1¼ cups sugar

2 teaspoons baking powder

2 tablespoons cardamom

Zest of 1 large orange

½ teaspoon fine sea salt

3 large eggs

1 cup plain yogurt

½ cup whole milk

Confectioners' sugar, for dusting

1. Preheat the oven to 350°F. Coat a 12-cup, fluted cast-iron tube pan with nonstick cooking spray. Place the flour, sugar, baking powder, cardamom, orange zest, and salt in a large bowl and whisk to combine.

2. Place the eggs, yogurt, and milk in a separate bowl and stir to combine. Add the wet mixture to the dry mixture and stir with a wooden spoon until just combined.

3. Pour the batter into the tube pan, place the pan in the oven, and bake until the cake is golden brown and a toothpick inserted into the center comes out clean, about 50 minutes.

4. Remove the cake from the oven, immediately remove the cake from the pan, and let it cool on a wire rack.

5. Dust the cake with confectioners' sugar and enjoy.

YIELD: *4 Servings* / ACTIVE TIME: 30 Minutes / TOTAL TIME: 2 Hours

Zeppole with Lemon Curd

If so inclined, fill the zeppole with the Meyer Lemon Curd. To do this, poke a hole in the zeppole once they have cooled, place the Meyer Lemon Curd in a piping bag, insert the tip into the hole, and squeeze the desired amount into the zeppole.

1½ cups all-purpose flour

1 tablespoon plus 1 teaspoon baking powder

¼ teaspoon fine sea salt

2 eggs

2 tablespoons sugar

2 cups ricotta cheese

Zest of 1 orange

1 cup milk

1 teaspoon pure vanilla extract

Canola oil, as needed

¼ cup confectioners' sugar, for dusting

Meyer Lemon Curd (see page 210)

1. Sift the flour, baking powder, and salt into a bowl. Set the mixture aside.

2. Place the eggs and sugar in a separate bowl and whisk to combine. Add the ricotta, whisk to incorporate, and then stir in the orange zest, milk, and vanilla.

3. Gradually incorporate the dry mixture into the wet mixture until it comes together as a smooth batter. Place the batter in the refrigerator and chill for 1 hour.

4. Add canola oil to a cast-iron Dutch oven until it is about 2 inches deep and warm it to 350°F. Drop tablespoons of the batter into the hot oil, taking care not to crowd the pot, and fry until the zeppole are golden brown. Transfer the fried zeppole to a paper towel–lined plate and dust them with confectioners' sugar.

5. To serve, spread some Meyer Lemon Curd on each serving plate and top with 2 or 3 zeppole.

APPENDIX

Cured Egg Yolks

1½ cups kosher salt

½ cup sugar

4 egg yolks

1. Combine the salt and sugar in a wide bowl. Using a spoon, create four small wells in the mixture, one for each yolk.

2. Carefully place each yolk into its own well. Spoon the mixture over the yolks until they are covered completely.

3. Cover the bowl with plastic wrap, place it in the refrigerator, and let the egg yolks cure for 3 days.

4. Remove the yolks from the mixture, rinse under cold water, and slice before serving.

Tahini & Yogurt Sauce

¾ cup full-fat Greek yogurt

1 garlic clove, minced

3 tablespoons tahini paste

Juice of 1 lemon

½ teaspoon cumin

Salt and pepper, to taste

1 tablespoon black sesame seeds

1 tablespoon extra-virgin olive oil

1. Place the yogurt, garlic, tahini, lemon juice, and cumin in a small bowl and whisk to combine.

2. Season the sauce with salt and pepper, add the sesame seeds and olive oil, and whisk until incorporated. Use immediately or store in the refrigerator until needed.

Sos Ti Malice

---

1 teaspoon extra-virgin olive oil

1 small onion, sliced

2 Scotch bonnet chile peppers or 2 habanero chile peppers, stems and seeds removed, sliced

½ small red bell pepper, sliced

3 garlic cloves, sliced

Salt and pepper, to taste

2 tablespoons tomato paste

2 tablespoons apple cider vinegar

1 tablespoon fresh lime juice

1 cup water, plus more as needed

1. Place the olive oil in a medium saucepan and warm it over medium heat. Add the onion, chiles, bell pepper, and garlic, season with salt and pepper, and cook for about 5 minutes.

2. Add the remaining ingredients and bring to a boil. Reduce the heat so that the mixture simmers and cook for about 20 minutes.

3. Transfer the mixture to a blender and puree on high until smooth. Add water as desired to achieve the right consistency.

4. Taste the hot sauce, adjust the seasoning as necessary, and use immediately or store it in the refrigerator.

Sweet Potato Puree

½ cup wood chips

2 sweet potatoes, peeled and chopped

1 Yukon Gold potato, peeled and chopped

2 teaspoons kosher salt, plus more to taste

½ cup heavy cream

2 tablespoons unsalted butter

1. Preheat the oven to 250°F. Place the wood chips in a cast-iron skillet and place the pan over high heat. When the wood chips start to smoke, place the skillet in a deep roasting pan. Set the sweet potatoes and potato in the roasting pan (not in the skillet) and cover the roasting pan with aluminum foil. Place in the oven for 30 minutes.

2. While the potatoes are smoking in the oven, bring water to a boil in a large saucepan. Remove the potatoes from the oven, salt the boiling water, and add the potatoes. Cook until they are fork-tender, 20 to 25 minutes. Drain, place in a mixing bowl, and add the remaining ingredients. Mash until smooth, season with salt, and serve immediately.

Pickled Ramps

½ cup champagne vinegar

½ cup water

¼ cup sugar

1½ teaspoons kosher salt

¼ teaspoon fennel seeds

¼ teaspoon coriander seeds

⅛ teaspoon red pepper flakes

10 small ramp bulbs

1. Place all of the ingredients, except for the ramps, in a small saucepan and bring the mixture to a boil over medium heat.

2. Add the ramps, reduce the heat, and simmer for 1 minute. Transfer the ramps and the brine to a mason jar, cover it with plastic wrap, and let the ramps cool completely before serving or storing in the refrigerator.

Labneh

4 cups full-fat Greek yogurt

½ teaspoon fine sea salt

1 tablespoon extra-virgin olive oil

2 teaspoons za'atar seasoning

1. Place the yogurt in a large bowl and season it with the salt; the salt helps pull out excess whey, giving you a creamier, thicker labneh.

2. Place a fine-mesh strainer on top of a medium-sized bowl. Line the strainer with cheesecloth or a linen towel, letting a few inches hang over the side of the strainer. Spoon the seasoned yogurt into the cheesecloth and gently wrap the sides over the top of the yogurt, protecting it from being exposed to air in the refrigerator.

3. Store everything in the refrigerator for 24 to 48 hours, discarding the whey halfway through if the bowl beneath the strainer becomes too full.

4. Remove the labneh from the cheesecloth and store it in an airtight container.

5. To serve, drizzle the olive oil over the labneh and sprinkle the za'atar on top.

Baozi Wrappers

1 tablespoon active dry yeast

1½ cups water, at room temperature

¼ cup canola oil, plus more as needed

¼ cup plus 1 teaspoon sugar

½ teaspoon kosher salt

4 teaspoons baking powder

2 cups all-purpose flour, plus more as needed

2 cups bread flour

1. Place the yeast, water, and canola oil in a small bowl, gently stir, and let the mixture sit until it is foamy, about 10 minutes.

2. Place the sugar, salt, baking powder, and flours in a food processor and pulse for 15 seconds to combine. With the food processor running on low speed, add the yeast mixture and work the mixture until it comes together as a slightly tacky dough. Transfer the dough to a flour-dusted work surface and knead until it is smooth, about 3 minutes. Place the dough in a bowl coated with canola oil, cover the bowl with a kitchen towel, and let the dough rise in a naturally warm place until it has doubled in size, about 30 minutes.

3. Place the dough on a flour-dusted work surface, cut it in half, and roll each piece into a log. Cut each log into 8 pieces. Roll each piece into a 4-inch circle and fill as desired. Cover the unrolled pieces of dough with a kitchen towel so that they do not dry out.

Dashi Stock

8 cups cold water

2 oz. kombu

1 cup bonito flakes

1. Place the water and the kombu in a medium saucepan. Soak the kombu for 20 minutes, remove it, and score it gently with a knife.

2. Return the kombu to the saucepan and bring to a boil. Remove the kombu as soon as the water boils, so that the stock doesn't become bitter.

3. Add the bonito flakes to the water and return it to a boil. Turn off the heat and let the mixture stand.

4. Strain the stock through a fine sieve. Use immediately or let it cool before using or storing.

Okonomiyaki Sauce

3 tablespoons Worcestershire sauce

3½ tablespoons ketchup

2 tablespoons oyster sauce

1½ tablespoons light brown sugar

1. Place all of the ingredients in a bowl and whisk until the brown sugar has dissolved and the mixture is well combined.

2. Use immediately or store in the refrigerator.

Recado Rojo

3½ oz. achoite paste

14 tablespoons fresh lime juice

14 tablespoons orange juice

7 tablespoons grapefruit juice

1 teaspoon dried Mexican oregano

1 teaspoon dried marjoram

1 habanero chile pepper, stems and seeds removed

5 garlic cloves

1 cinnamon stick, grated

Salt, to taste

1. Place the achiote paste and juices in a bowl and let the mixture sit for 15 minutes.

2. Place the mixture and the remaining ingredients in a blender and puree until smooth.

3. Taste, adjust the seasoning as needed, and use as desired.

Meyer Lemon Curd

¾ cup fresh Meyer lemon juice

4 eggs

¾ cup sugar

¼ teaspoon kosher salt

¼ teaspoon pure vanilla extract

½ cup unsalted butter, softened

1. Fill a small saucepan halfway with water and bring it to a gentle simmer.

2. Place the lemon juice in a small saucepan and warm it over low heat.

3. Combine the eggs, sugar, salt, and vanilla in a metal mixing bowl. Place the bowl over the simmering water and whisk the mixture continually until it is 135°F on an instant-read thermometer.

4. When the lemon juice comes to a simmer, gradually add it to the egg mixture while whisking constantly.

5. When all of the lemon juice has been incorporated, whisk the curd until it has thickened and is 155°F. Remove the bowl from heat, add the butter, and stir until thoroughly incorporated.

6. Transfer the curd to a mason jar and let it cool. Once cool, store the curd in the refrigerator, where it will keep for up to 2 weeks.

Beef Stock

2 lbs. yellow onions, chopped

1 lb. carrots, chopped

1 lb. celery, chopped

5 lbs. beef bones

2 tablespoons tomato paste

16 cups water

1 cup red wine

1 tablespoon black peppercorns

2 bay leaves

3 sprigs of fresh thyme

3 sprigs of fresh parsley

1. Preheat the oven to 375ºF. Divide the onions, carrots, and celery between two baking sheets in even layers. Place the beef bones on top, place the pans in the oven, and roast the vegetables and beef bones for 45 minutes.

2. Spread the tomato paste over the beef bones and then roast for another 5 minutes.

3. Remove the pans from the oven, transfer the vegetables and beef bones to a stockpot, and cover with the water. Bring to a boil.

4. Reduce the heat so that the stock simmers. Deglaze the pans with the red wine, scraping up any browned bits from the bottom. Stir the liquid into the stock, add the remaining ingredients, and cook, skimming any impurities that rise to the surface, until the stock has reduced by half and the flavor is to your liking, about 6 hours.

5. Strain the stock and either use immediately or let it cool completely before storing in the refrigerator.

Chicken Stock

10 leftover chicken bones

32 cups cold water

¼ cup white wine

1 onion, chopped

1 celery stalk, chopped

1 carrot, chopped

2 bay leaves

10 sprigs of fresh parsley

10 sprigs of fresh thyme

1 teaspoon black peppercorns

Salt, to taste

1. Preheat the oven to 400°F. Place the chicken bones on a baking sheet, place them in the oven, and roast them until they are caramelized, about 1 hour.

2. Remove the chicken bones from the oven and place them in a stock-pot. Cover them with the water and bring to a boil, skimming to remove any impurities that rise to the surface.

3. Deglaze the baking sheet with the white wine, scraping up any browned bits from the bottom. Stir the liquid into the stock, add the remaining ingredients, and reduce the heat so that the stock simmers. Simmer the stock until it has reduced by three-quarters and the flavor is to your liking, about 6 hours, skimming the surface as needed.

4. Strain the stock and either use immediately or let it cool completely and store it in the refrigerator.

Salsa de Chiltomate

8½ oz. Roma tomatoes, halved

2 habanero chile peppers

1 small white onion, quartered

4 garlic cloves, unpeeled

2 tablespoons extra-virgin olive oil

Salt, to taste

Juice of 1 lime

1. Preheat the oven to 450ºF. Line a baking sheet with parchment paper, place the tomatoes, chiles, onion, and garlic on it, and place it in the oven.

2. Roast until the vegetables are charred all over, checking every 5 minutes or so and removing them as they become ready.

3. Peel the garlic cloves, remove the stem and seeds from the habanero, and place the roasted vegetables in a blender. Puree until smooth.

4. Place the olive oil in a medium saucepan and warm it over medium-high heat. Carefully pour the puree into the pan, reduce the heat, and simmer until the salsa has reduced slightly and the flavor is to your liking, 15 to 20 minutes.

5. Season with salt, stir in the lime juice, and let the salsa cool. Taste, adjust the seasoning as necessary, and serve.

Corn Tortillas

1 lb. masa harina

1½ tablespoons kosher salt

3 cups warm filtered water, plus more as needed

1. In the work bowl of a stand mixer fitted with the paddle attachment, combine the masa harina and salt. With the mixer on low speed, slowly begin to add the water. The mixture should come together as a soft, smooth dough. You want the masa to be moist enough so that when a small ball of it is pressed flat in your hands, the edges do not crack. Also, it should not stick to your hands when you peel it off your palm.

2. Let the masa rest for 10 minutes and check the hydration again. You may need to add more water, depending on environmental conditions.

3. Warm a cast-iron skillet over high heat. Portion the masa into 1-ounce balls and cover them with a damp linen towel.

4. Line a tortilla press with two 8-inch circles of plastic. You can use a grocery store bag, a resealable bag, or even a standard kitchen trash bag as a source for the plastic. Place a masa ball in the center of one circle and gently push down on it with the palm of one hand to flatten. Place the other plastic circle on top and then close the tortilla press, applying firm, even pressure to flatten the masa into a round tortilla.

5. Open the tortilla press and remove the top layer of plastic. Carefully pick up the tortilla and remove the bottom piece of plastic.

6. Gently lay the tortilla flat in the pan, taking care to not wrinkle it. Cook for 15 to 30 seconds, until the edge begins to lift up slightly. Turn the tortilla over and let it cook for 30 to 45 seconds before turning it over one last time. If the hydration of the masa was correct and the heat is high enough, the tortilla should puff up and inflate. Remove the tortilla from the pan and store in a tortilla warmer lined with a linen towel. Repeat until all of the prepared masa has been made into tortillas.

Seeded Buttermilk Buns

½ cup buttermilk

2 cups all-purpose flour, plus more as needed

¾ teaspoon fine sea salt

¾ teaspoon active dry yeast

2½ tablespoons sugar

2 eggs

4 tablespoons unsalted butter, softened, plus more as needed

1 teaspoon milk

¼ cup mixed seeds (white and black sesame seeds, flaxseeds, poppy seeds)

1. Place the buttermilk in the work bowl of a stand mixer fitted with the dough hook. Add the flour, salt, yeast, sugar, 1 egg, and the butter and mix on low until combined.

2. Raise the speed to high and mix until the mixture comes together as a smooth, elastic dough.

3. Coat a large bowl with butter, form the dough into a ball, and place it in the bowl. Cover the bowl with plastic wrap and let the dough rise in a naturally warm spot until it has doubled in size, about 30 minutes.

4. Line a baking sheet with parchment paper. Place the dough on a flour-dusted work surface and cut it into 3½-oz. pieces. Roll them into tight balls and place them on the baking sheet, leaving at least 2½ inches of space between them. Cover the buns with a kitchen towel and place them in a naturally warm spot until they have doubled in size, about 30 minutes.

5. Preheat the oven to 325°F.

6. Place the remaining egg and the milk in a bowl and whisk to combine. Brush the buns with the egg wash and sprinkle the seeds over the top.

7. Place the buns in the oven and bake until they are golden brown, 20 to 25 minutes.

8. Remove the buns from the oven and let them cool before serving.

Pickled Carrots

2 cups apple cider vinegar

¼ cup sugar

2 teaspoons coriander seeds

1 teaspoon fennel seeds

½ teaspoon red pepper flakes

½ teaspoon fine sea salt

2 large carrots, peeled and sliced thin

1. Place all of the ingredients, except for the carrots, in a small saucepan and bring to a boil.

2. Place the carrots in a mason jar and pour the brine over them.

3. Set the pickled carrots aside and let them cool completely before serving or storing in the refrigerator.

YIELD: 1 Cup / **ACTIVE TIME:** 5 Minutes / **TOTAL TIME:** 5 Minutes

Epis

8 scallions, trimmed

½ bunch of fresh parsley

1½ oz. garlic cloves, chopped

¼ large onion, chopped

1 tablespoon fresh thyme

¼ red bell pepper

¼ green bell pepper

¼ yellow bell pepper

¼ orange bell pepper

¼ habanero chile pepper

2 tablespoons extra-virgin olive oil

Juice of ½ lime

Salt, to taste

1. Place all of the ingredients in a blender and pulse until the mixture is a coarse paste.

2. Taste, adjust the seasoning as necessary, and pulse until smooth.

3. Use the epis immediately or store it in the refrigerator.

Harissa

1 head of garlic, halved at the equator

2 tablespoons extra-virgin olive oil

2 bell peppers

2 tablespoons coriander seeds

6 chiles de árbol

3 pasilla chile peppers

2 shallots, halved

2 teaspoons kosher salt

1. Preheat the oven to 400°F. Place the garlic in a piece of aluminum foil, drizzle half of the olive oil over it, and seal the foil closed.

2. Place the garlic on a baking sheet with the bell peppers and place it in the oven. Roast until the garlic is very tender and the peppers are charred all over. Remove them from the oven and let them cool.

3. While the garlic and peppers are cooling, place the coriander seeds in a dry skillet and toast them over medium heat, shaking the pan frequently. Transfer the coriander seeds to a blender along with the remaining ingredients, including the remaining olive oil.

4. Squeeze the roasted garlic cloves into the blender. Remove the skin, seeds, and stems from the roasted peppers and place the flesh in the blender.

5. Puree until the harissa paste has the desired texture and use immediately or store it in the refrigerator.

Pickled Red Onion

½ cup apple cider vinegar

½ cup water

2 tablespoons kosher salt

2 tablespoons sugar

1 red onion, sliced thin

1. Place the vinegar, water, salt, and sugar in a saucepan and bring to a boil, stirring to dissolve the salt and sugar.

2. Place the onion in a bowl, pour the brine over it, and let it cool completely.

3. Transfer the onion and brine to a mason jar and let it cool completely before serving or storing in the refrigerator.

Cranberry Mostarda

½ cup dried cranberries, chopped

1 teaspoon diced shallot

2 teaspoons whole-grain mustard

1 tablespoon chopped fresh parsley

2 teaspoons sliced fresh chives

1½ tablespoons extra-virgin olive oil

1 teaspoon honey

2 teaspoons sherry vinegar

1. Place all of the ingredients in a small bowl and stir to combine.

2. Taste the mostarda, adjust the seasoning as necessary, and either use immediately or store it in the refrigerator.

Crispy Kale

½ bunch of kale

3 tablespoons extra-virgin olive oil

Salt and pepper, to taste

1. Preheat the oven to 350°F. Remove the leaves of the kale from the stems and tear the leaves. Place them in a bowl, add the olive oil, and season with salt and pepper. Toss to combine.

2. Place the kale on a baking sheet and place it in the oven. Bake until the kale is crispy, 6 to 8 minutes.

3. Remove the kale chips from the oven and either use immediately or store them in an airtight container.

Braised Fennel

2 tablespoons extra-virgin olive oil

2 fennel bulbs, trimmed and halved

½ cup white wine

Zest and juice of ½ lemon

2 cups Chicken Stock (see page 212)

1 tablespoon honey

1 radicchio, core removed, sliced thin

Salt and pepper, to taste

1. Place the olive oil in a Dutch oven and warm it over medium-high heat. Add the fennel and cook until it is golden brown on both sides, 6 to 8 minutes.

2. Add the white wine and cook until it has almost evaporated, about 3 minutes, scraping up any browned bits from the bottom of the Dutch oven.

3. Add the lemon zest, lemon juice, stock, and honey, bring to a simmer, and cover the pot. Simmer until the fennel is tender, about 10 minutes. Remove the fennel from the pot with a slotted spoon and place it in a bowl.

4. Add the radicchio to the Dutch oven and cook over medium heat, stirring frequently, until it has softened, about 5 minutes.

5. Place the radicchio on top of the fennel, season the dish with salt and pepper, and serve.

Balsamic Glaze

1 cup balsamic vinegar

¼ cup brown sugar

1. Place the vinegar and brown sugar in a small saucepan and bring the mixture to a boil.

2. Reduce the heat to medium-low and simmer for 8 to 10 minutes, stirring frequently, until the mixture has thickened.

3. Remove the pan from heat and let the glaze cool for 15 minutes before using.

Scallion Cream Cheese

½ cup cream cheese, softened

2 tablespoons minced scallions

½ teaspoon kosher salt

¼ teaspoon white pepper

1 teaspoon lemon zest

1. Place all of the ingredients in a bowl and stir to combine.

2. Use the cream cheese immediately or store it in the refrigerator.

YIELD: 4 Servings / ACTIVE TIME: 20 Minutes / TOTAL TIME: 40 Minutes

Braised Cauliflower

¼ cup extra-virgin olive oil

1 head of cauliflower, trimmed and halved through the stem

Salt and pepper, to taste

2 garlic cloves, minced

⅛ teaspoon red pepper flakes

1 teaspoon sumac

½ cup white wine

1 bay leaf

6 to 8 cups Chicken Stock (see page 212)

2 scallions, trimmed and sliced on a bias, for garnish

1. Place the olive oil in a Dutch oven and warm it over medium heat. Season the cauliflower with salt and pepper, place it in the Dutch oven, and cook until golden brown all over, about 6 minutes, turning it as necessary. Remove the cauliflower from the pot and set it aside.

2. Add the garlic, red pepper flakes, and sumac and cook, stirring continually, for 1 minute. Add the wine and cook until the alcohol has been cooked off, about 2 minutes. Add the bay leaf, return the cauliflower to the pot, and add stock until the cauliflower is covered. Bring the mixture to a simmer and cook until the stem of the cauliflower is tender, about 10 minutes.

3. Transfer the cauliflower to a serving dish, garnish with the scallions, and enjoy.

Honey-Glazed Carrots

5 lbs. carrots, peeled

4 tablespoons unsalted butter

⅓ cup orange juice

1 tablespoon buckwheat honey

1½ teaspoons kosher salt

2 tablespoons fresh lemon juice

⅛ teaspoon cayenne pepper

1. Place the carrots, butter, orange juice, honey, and salt in a saucepan, cover the pan, and cook over medium heat until the carrots are tender, about 10 minutes.

2. Uncover the pan and continue to cook the carrots, stirring occasionally, until the sauce reduces slightly, about 10 minutes.

3. Remove the pan from heat, stir in the lemon juice and cayenne, and transfer the carrots and sauce to a serving dish. Enjoy immediately.

YIELD: 4 Servings / **ACTIVE TIME:** 15 Minutes / **TOTAL TIME:** 50 Minutes

Roasted Root Vegetables

½ lb. parsnips, trimmed, peeled, and cut into 1-inch cubes

1 celeriac, trimmed, peeled, and cut into 1-inch cubes

½ lb. Brussels sprouts, trimmed and halved

1 lb. new potatoes

6 shallots, peeled and quartered

4 garlic cloves, minced

2 teaspoons fresh thyme

1 teaspoon chopped fresh rosemary

1 tablespoon honey

6 tablespoons extra-virgin olive oil

Salt and pepper, to taste

2 tablespoons chopped fresh parsley

1 tablespoon capers, drained and chopped

Zest and juice of 1 lemon

1. Preheat the oven to 425°F. Place the parsnips, celeriac, Brussels sprouts, potatoes, shallots, garlic, thyme, rosemary, honey, and ¼ cup of the olive oil in a mixing bowl and toss to coat. Season the mixture with salt and pepper and spread the mixture on a baking sheet in a single layer.

2. Place the vegetables in the oven and roast until golden brown and tender, 30 to 35 minutes. Remove the vegetables from the oven and let them cool.

3. Place the parsley, capers, lemon zest, lemon juice, and remaining olive oil in a mixing bowl and whisk to combine.

4. Drizzle the sauce over the roasted vegetables, toss to coat, and enjoy.

Caper Cream

2 tablespoons unsalted butter

2 tablespoons diced shallot

2 garlic cloves, minced

2 tablespoons capers

2 tablespoons white wine

1 cup heavy cream

1 tablespoon fresh lemon juice

Salt, to taste

1. Place the butter in a small saucepan and melt it over medium heat. Add the shallot and garlic and cook, stirring continually, for 1 minute. Add the capers and wine and cook until the wine has evaporated.

2. Add the cream and cook, stirring continually, until it has reduced by half.

3. Add the lemon juice, taste, and season with salt. Remove the pan from heat and let the caper cream cool before using.

Pickled Kumquats

½ lb. kumquats, halved and seeded

2 cups rice vinegar

2 tablespoons sugar

½ teaspoon kosher salt

1. Place the kumquats in a mason jar.

2. Place the vinegar, sugar, and salt in a small saucepan and bring to a boil, stirring to dissolve the sugar and salt.

3. Pour the brine over the kumquats and let them cool completely before using or storing in the refrigerator.

Red Chermoula Sauce

Pinch of saffron threads

¼ cup Harissa (see page 218)

½ cup extra-virgin olive oil

1 tablespoon chopped preserved lemons

2 teaspoons kosher salt

1 tablespoon smoked paprika

1 teaspoon cumin powder

2 teaspoons fresh lemon juice

2 tablespoons chopped fresh cilantro

1 tablespoon chopped fresh parsley

1 tablespoon sliced fresh chives

1. Using a mortar and pestle or food processor, combine all of the ingredients, except for the herbs, until the desired consistency has been achieved.

2. Add the herbs and stir until well combined.

3. Taste the sauce, adjust the seasoning as necessary, and use immediately or store it in the refrigerator.

YIELD: 2 Cups / **ACTIVE TIME:** 5 Minutes / **TOTAL TIME:** 30 Minutes

Salsa Macha

1 cup raw unsalted peanuts

2 cups extra-virgin olive oil

5 garlic cloves, sliced

1 shallot, sliced

¼ cup sunflower seeds

½ teaspoon cumin seeds

½ teaspoon fennel seeds

1 tablespoon white sesame seeds

1 tablespoon black sesame seeds

1 tablespoon coriander seeds

2 ancho chile peppers, stems and seeds removed

2 guajillo chile peppers, stems and seeds removed

5 chiles de árbol, stems and seeds removed

1 teaspoon apple cider vinegar

Salt, to taste

1. Place the peanuts and olive oil in a medium saucepan and cook over medium-low heat, stirring occasionally, until the peanuts start to brown, 10 to 15 minutes.

2. Add the remaining ingredients and cook, stirring occasionally, until the garlic and shallot have browned and all of the excess moisture has evaporated. Remove the pan from heat and let the mixture cool slightly.

3. Strain the mixture, reserving the oil. Using a mortar and pestle, grind the solids coarsely. Stir in the oil, season the salsa with salt, and use as desired.

Arugula Chimichurri

½ cup chopped arugula

1½ teaspoons chopped fresh oregano

1 small shallot, diced

1 small garlic clove, minced

2 tablespoons red wine vinegar

Salt and pepper, to taste

½ cup extra-virgin olive oil

1. Place all of the ingredients, except for the olive oil, in a mixing bowl and whisk to combine.

2. While whisking continually, slowly stream in the olive oil until it has emulsified.

3. Taste the chimichurri, adjust the seasoning as necessary, and either use immediately or store it in the refrigerator.

Jerk Spice Blend

1 tablespoon onion powder

1 tablespoon garlic powder

1 tablespoon dried thyme

1 tablespoon adobo seasoning

2 teaspoons sazon

2 teaspoons cayenne pepper

2 teaspoons kosher salt

2 teaspoons black pepper

1 tablespoon allspice

1 tablespoon paprika

1 teaspoon red pepper flakes

1 teaspoon cumin

2 teaspoons cinnamon

½ teaspoon nutmeg

1 teaspoon ground cloves

1 teaspoon ground ginger

1 cup Epis (see page 217)

1 tablespoon browning sauce

1. Place all of the ingredients in a mixing bowl, stir to combine, and use immediately or store in an airtight container.

Fennel Pesto

¾ cup pine nuts

1 cup chopped fennel greens

½ cup fresh parsley

10 fresh mint leaves

1 teaspoon fine sea salt

½ teaspoon black pepper

1 teaspoon fresh lemon juice

Zest of 1 lemon

¼ cup canola oil

1 tablespoon extra-virgin olive oil

1. Preheat the oven to 350°F. Place the pine nuts on a baking sheet and place them in the oven. Toast the pine nuts until they are fragrant and browned, about 6 minutes. Remove the pine nuts from the oven and set them aside.

2. Place the toasted pine nuts and all of the remaining ingredients, except for the oils, in a food processor and blitz to combine. With the food processor running, slowly stream in the oils until they have emulsified.

3. Taste the pesto, adjust the seasoning as necessary, and use immediately or store it in the refrigerator.

Tzatziki

1 cup full-fat Greek yogurt

¾ cup deseeded and minced cucumber

1 garlic clove, minced

Juice from 1 lemon wedge

Salt and white pepper, to taste

Fresh dill, finely chopped, to taste

1. Place the yogurt, cucumber, garlic, and lemon juice in a mixing bowl and stir to combine. Taste and season with salt and pepper. Stir in the dill.

2. Place in the refrigerator and chill for 1 hour before serving.

YIELD: 4 Servings / ACTIVE TIME: 30 Minutes / TOTAL TIME: 1 Hour and 30 Minutes

Couscous-Stuffed Tomatoes

4 tomatoes

2 teaspoons sugar

Salt and pepper, to taste

2 tablespoons plus 1 teaspoon extra-virgin olive oil

¼ cup panko

1 cup freshly grated Manchego cheese

1 onion, chopped

2 garlic cloves, minced

⅛ teaspoon red pepper flakes

4 cups baby spinach

¾ cup couscous

1½ cups Chicken Stock (see page 212)

2 tablespoons chopped Kalamata olives

2 teaspoons red wine vinegar

1. Preheat the oven to 350°F. Cut the top ½ inch off the tomatoes and scoop out their insides. Sprinkle the sugar and some salt into the tomatoes, turn them upside down, and place them on a wire rack. Let the tomatoes drain for 30 minutes.

2. Place 1 teaspoon of the olive oil in a large skillet and warm it over medium heat. Add the panko and cook, stirring continually, until it is golden brown, about 3 minutes. Remove the panko from the pan, place it in a bowl, and let it cool.

3. Stir half of the cheese into the cooled panko and set the mixture aside.

4. Place 1 tablespoon of the olive oil in a clean large skillet and warm it over medium-high heat. Add the onion and cook, stirring occasionally, until it has softened, about 5 minutes. Add the garlic and red pepper flakes and cook, stirring continually, for 1 minute.

5. Add the spinach and cook until it has wilted, about 2 minutes. Add the couscous and stock and bring the mixture to a simmer. Cover the pan, remove it from heat, and let it sit until the couscous is tender, about 7 minutes.

6. Fluff the couscous with a fork, add the olives, vinegar, and remaining cheese, and fold until incorporated. Season the stuffing with salt and pepper and set it aside.

7. Place the remaining olive oil in a baking dish. Add the tomatoes, cavities facing up, and fill them with the stuffing. Top with the toasted panko mixture and place the tomatoes in the oven. Roast until the tomatoes are tender, about 20 minutes.

8. Remove the tomatoes from the oven and let them cool slightly before enjoying.

YIELD: 1¼ Cups / **ACTIVE TIME:** 5 Minutes / **TOTAL TIME:** 5 Minutes

Tennessee Tartar Sauce

1 cup mayonnaise

½ teaspoon hot sauce

1 tablespoon sweet-and-spicy relish

¼ teaspoon garlic powder

1 tablespoon minced onion

2 tablespoons fresh lemon juice

Salt and pepper, to taste

1. Place all of the ingredients in a bowl, stir to combine, and use as desired.

Sour Cherry Glaze

1 cup sour cherry preserves

¼ cup Chicken Stock (see page 212)

2 tablespoons soy sauce

2 tablespoons spicy brown mustard

1. Place all of the ingredients in a saucepan and bring to a boil over medium-high heat.

2. Reduce the heat and simmer until the mixture has thickened and reduced by half. Use as desired.

Chicken & Waffle Dipping Sauce

¼ cup water

3 tablespoons fresh lemon juice

2 tablespoons maple syrup

2 tablespoons fish sauce

1 tablespoon soy sauce

2 fresh Thai bird or habanero peppers, thinly sliced

1. Combine the ingredients in a small bowl. Cover and refrigerate until ready to use.

Adobo Broth

2½ cups distilled white vinegar

1½ cups water

3 garlic cloves, finely minced

4 bay leaves

1½ teaspoons black peppercorns

1 teaspoon sugar

¼ cup soy sauce

½ teaspoon red pepper flakes

1 teaspoon salt

1. In a large pot, combine all the ingredients, cover with a tight-fitting lid, and bring to a simmer over medium heat.

2. Simmer for 5 minutes and use as desired.

Basic Brine

⅓ cup kosher salt

⅓ cup sugar

¼ cup juniper berries

2 tablespoons black peppercorns

4 bay leaves

1. Combine 4 cups water, the salt, sugar, juniper berries, peppercorns, and bay leaves in a pot and bring to a boil.

2. Stir until the salt and sugar dissolve, then remove from the heat and allow to cool completely before using. The brine will keep in the refrigerator for up to 2 weeks.

Spicy Mayo

1 cup mayonnaise

2 Thai chile peppers, minced

4 teaspoons fresh lime juice

1 teaspoon fish sauce

¼ teaspoon salt

1. Whisk together all the ingredients in a small bowl. Cover and refrigerate until ready to use.

YIELD: 6 Servings / **ACTIVE TIME:** 5 Minutes / **TOTAL TIME:** 30 Minutes

Pear, Ginger & Cilantro Slaw

1 Asian pear, cored and cut into matchsticks (about 1½ cups)

1 cup fresh bean sprouts

1 cup coarsely chopped fresh cilantro sprigs (leaves and tender stems)

1 tablespoon grated fresh ginger (use a Microplane)

1 teaspoon rice vinegar

1 teaspoon fish sauce

Kosher salt and freshly ground black pepper, to taste

1. Combine the pear, bean sprouts, cilantro, ginger, vinegar, and fish sauce in a medium bowl. Season to taste with salt and pepper.

2. Taste. Is it sweet and crunchy? Good. Let it rest for a bit in the refrigerator before using.

Pickled Peaches

12 large ripe peaches

3½ cups distilled white vinegar

3 cups water

2½ cups sugar

1 lemongrass stalk, bruised and chopped

1 tablespoon grated fresh ginger

15 black peppercorns

10 allspice berries

2 whole cloves

1 cinnamon stick

Pinch of ground mace

1. Bring a large pot of water to a boil over high heat. Make an ice bath with equal parts ice and water in a large bowl. Submerge the peaches in the boiling water for 1 minute. Remove and submerge them and stop the cooking. Peel the peaches and place them in a nonreactive heatproof container.

2. Combine all the remaining ingredients in a nonreactive saucepan and bring to a boil over medium-high heat, stirring to completely dissolve the sugar. Reduce the heat to low and simmer for 5 minutes.

3. Pour the hot pickling liquid over the peaches. Cool to room temperature, cover, and refrigerate for at least 1 week before eating to allow the peaches to cure. Tightly sealed, the peaches will keep for up to 2 months in the refrigerator.

YIELD: ½ Cup / **ACTIVE TIME:** 5 Minutes / **TOTAL TIME:** 25 Minutes

Macerated Shallot Vinaigrette

1 shallot, finely diced

2 tablespoons seasoned rice wine vinegar, or enough to just cover the shallots

¼ cup extra-virgin olive oil

2 to 3 twists of pepper

1. Combine the shallot and rice vinegar and allow them to macerate for at least 20 minutes, or up to overnight.

2. Whisk in the olive oil and pepper. You can store this in your refrigerator for up to a week, but you will get the freshest and brightest flavor if you use it within 24 hours.

Rhubarb Compote

3 cups chopped rhubarb (1-inch pieces)

⅔ cup sugar

1 teaspoon lemon zest

2 teaspoons fresh lemon juice

2 teaspoons cornstarch

1. In a medium heavy-bottomed saucepan, combine the rhubarb, sugar, lemon zest, lemon juice, and cornstarch.

2. Bring to a simmer over medium heat, stirring constantly until the rhubarb becomes tender and sauce-like, about 5 minutes.

3. Remove from the heat and allow to cool to room temperature. The compote will keep in the refrigerator for up to 1 week.

YIELD: 2 Cups / **ACTIVE TIME:** 5 Minutes / **TOTAL TIME:** 5 Minutes

Perfectly Whipped Cream

2 cups heavy cream

2 tablespoons confectioners' sugar

1 teaspoon vanilla extract

1. In a stand mixer or working by hand with a whisk, preferably with a chilled bowl, whip the cream with the sugar and vanilla on high speed until soft peaks form.

Conversion Table

Weights

1 oz. = 28 grams
2 oz. = 57 grams
4 oz. (¼ lb.) = 113 grams
8 oz. (½ lb.) = 227 grams
16 oz. (1 lb.) = 454 grams

Volume Measures

⅛ teaspoon = 0.6 ml
¼ teaspoon = 1.23 ml
½ teaspoon = 2.5 ml
1 teaspoon = 5 ml
1 tablespoon (3 teaspoons) = ½ fluid oz. = 15 ml
2 tablespoons = 1 fluid oz. = 29.5 ml
¼ cup (4 tablespoons) = 2 fluid oz. = 59 ml
⅓ cup (5⅓ tablespoons) = 2.7 fluid oz. = 80 ml
½ cup (8 tablespoons) = 4 fluid oz. = 120 ml
⅔ cup (10⅔ tablespoons) = 5.4 fluid oz. = 160 ml
¾ cup (12 tablespoons) = 6 fluid oz. = 180 ml
1 cup (16 tablespoons) = 8 fluid oz. = 240 ml

Temperature Equivalents

°F	°C	Gas Mark
225	110	¼
250	130	½
275	140	1
300	150	2
325	170	3
350	180	4
375	190	5
400	200	6
425	220	7
450	230	8
475	240	9
500	250	10

Length Measures

1/16 inch = 1.6 mm
⅛ inch = 3 mm
¼ inch = 6.35 mm
½ inch = 1.25 cm
¾ inch = 2 cm
1 inch = 2.5 cm

Credits

Index

About Cider Mill Press
Book Publishers

Good ideas ripen with time. From seed to harvest,
Cider Mill Press brings fine reading, information, and entertainment
together between the covers of its creatively crafted books.
Our Cider Mill bears fruit twice a year, publishing a new
crop of titles each spring and fall.

"Where Good Books Are Ready for Press"
501 Nelson Place
Nashville, Tennessee 37214

cidermillpress.com